NAVY SEAL SELF-DISCIPLINE:

HOW TO BECOME THE TOUGHEST WARRIOR

SELF-CONFIDENCE, SELF AWARENESS, SELF-CONTROL AND MENTAL TOUGHNESS

Fourth Edition

Table of Contents

INTRODUCTION:

CHAPTER 1: WHO ARE THE NAVY SEALS?

CHAPTER 2: NAVY SEALS TRAINING

CHAPTER 3: WHY SHOULD YOU TRAIN LIKE A NAVY SEAL?

CHAPTER 4: FITNESS

CHAPTER 5: COURAGE

CHAPTER 6: RESILIENCE

CHAPTER 7: MENTAL FITNESS

CHAPTER 8: CROSS FIT TRAINING

CHAPTER 9: SWIMMING TRAINING

CHAPTER 10: RUNNING TRAINING

CHAPTER 11: YOGA TRAINING

CHAPTER 12: MEDITATION BASICS

CHAPTER 13: MEDITATION ATMOSPHERE

CHAPTER 14: MINDFULNESS TECHNIQUES

CHAPTER 15: GENERAL TIPS

CHAPTER 16: SEAL TRAINING FAQs

CHAPTER 17: SITUATIONAL AWARENESS

CHAPTER 18: NUTRITION

KEY HIGHLIGHTS

CONCLUSION:

Instant Access to Free Book Package!

© **Copyright 2016 - All rights reserved.**

In no way is it legal to reproduce, duplicate, or transmit any part of this document in either electronic means or in printed format. Recording of this publication is strictly prohibited and any storage of this document is not allowed unless with written permission from the publisher. All rights reserved.

The information provided herein is stated to be truthful and consistent, in that any liability, in terms of inattention or otherwise, by any usage or abuse of any policies, processes, or directions contained within is the solitary and utter responsibility of the recipient reader. Under no circumstances will any legal responsibility or blame be held against the publisher for any reparation, damages, or monetary loss due to the information herein, either directly or indirectly.
Respective authors own all copyrights not held by the publisher.

Legal Notice:
This book is copyright protected. This is only for personal use. You cannot amend, distribute, sell, use, quote or paraphrase any part or the content within this book without the consent of the author or copyright owner. Legal action will be pursued if this is breached.

Disclaimer Notice:
Please note the information contained within this document is for educational and entertainment purposes only. Every attempt has been made to provide accurate, up to date and reliable complete information. No warranties of any kind are expressed or implied. Readers acknowledge that the author is not engaging in the rendering of legal, financial, medical or professional advice.

By reading this document, the reader agrees that under no circumstances are we responsible for any losses, direct or indirect, which are incurred as a result of the use of information contained within this document, including, but not limited to, —errors, omissions, or inaccuracies.

INTRODUCTION:

Navy SEALs are some of the most elite fighters in the world. Just how good? Consider the people who were able to finally neutralize Osama bin Laden. Who were those people? Navy SEALs!

But of course, Navy SEALs are known for much more than that. There are many different stories that portray the excellence, abilities, and power of these Special Forces men. And while they live and operate in a world that's much, much different than ours, we can learn a lot from them in terms of success and making the most out of life. And this is what it is about: training like a Navy Seal for optimal personal success. In this book, you'll read about how to mentally, physically, emotionally and nutritionally train like Navy SEALs.

Given that the nature of their work often entails the most difficult circumstances an individual can face in life, it is only logical that those who excel in the SEALs can get most other things down to an art. As you will learn in this book, the skills and wisdom obtained through their excruciating training can be more than applied in many different walks of life. In fact, by propelling yourself towards the SEALs level of training and exercise, you will be able to harness that which is most beneficial, yet not be burdened by some of the inherent difficulties that come with the actual job and duty.

Furthermore, gaining some insight and understanding of the hardships these men must surmount will also put things in perspective for you. Starting with their training, over the high-risk missions they are tasked with, all the way to the strain that this calling may put on their personal and family life, you will begin to see just how many hurdles life throws their way. It will become increasingly apparent that it takes a special caliber of man, and an even more unique form of training, to be able to overcome the trials and tribulations that come with a Navy SEAL's chosen way of life.

As we progress through this book, we will touch upon some real life stories and missions on the side as we go, while we try to paint the picture of just what it means to train on this level. It isn't for the faint at heart and the road to get there isn't an easy one.

While chances are you won't be nowhere near at par with the kinds of trainings that Navy SEALs do as well as their physical, emotional, and mental abilities, you can use many of the principles they use to attain a similar status – and stay there – in order to achieve peak performance. So if you're ready to become finely honed like Navy SEALs, turn the page and let's go.

Please feel free to share this book with your friends and family. Please also take the time to write a short review on Amazon to share your thoughts.

CHAPTER 1: WHO ARE THE NAVY SEALS?

Navy SEALs are a group of men who belong to the United States Navy's sea, air and land team, which was established under the orders of President John F. Kennedy back in 1962. They're an elite, small group of maritime military force specialists that engage in what is known as unconventional warfare. The types of missions that they carry out are high impact, small in unit size and clandestine, which aren't possible with higher profile and larger-sized forces like submarines, jets, tanks and ships. They also execute ground-based special reconnaissance missions on important military targets for eventual attack by bigger and more conventional forces. They're the Navy, Air Force, and Army Special Forces' units of choice for such operations – particularly those that start with and end in bodies of water like coastlines, deltas, swamps, oceans and rivers - because Navy SEALs can expertly navigate relatively shallow bodies of water like the Persian Gulf coast line, where submarines and large ships can't enter due to limited depth.

In other words, the SEALs are often the very tip of the spear in military operations throughout the globe. Whether it is sabotage, reconnaissance or apprehension/neutralization of high-value targets, SEALs will generally find themselves going in first to lay the groundwork for subsequent large-scale operations, which means the probability of them running into overwhelming odds is quite real. This is the reason why the tactical prowess and readiness of the men in the Navy SEALs must be above and beyond that of any potential foe.

While the Navy SEALs belong to the United States' naval unit, they're expertly trained to execute missions in all types of terrains, be it in water, air, or land. It's because of such specialized training and skills that they are named as such – SEALs. More than just operating in practically any terrain, they're also trained to execute critical missions even under the most extreme climates such as humid jungles, freezing winters, and scorching deserts.

The Navy SEALs have demonstrated this flexibility many times since their formation. With engagements in Vietnam, South America, Middle East, Europe and on the home front, just to name a few, they have successfully carried out their missions no matter the environment or the objective, thus fully living up to their assigned purpose.

In addition to their deeds and proven record, the Navy SEAL creed, or ethos, also gives us a clear idea of how dedicated these men are as well as just how high the standards they uphold really are. We often may not get a glimpse of their achievements due to the shroud of secrecy that surrounds them and their missions. However, those stories which we do get wind of, coupled with their official codex they swear to adhere to, are more than enough to recognize and stand in awe of their valor and professionalism.

THE NAVY SEALS ETHOS[1]

If you want to get a clearer picture of what these men are about more than just conducting highly covert missions that no one in their right frame of mind will volunteer to do, read the following, which is the official Navy SEALs ethos:

> "In times of war or uncertainty there is a special breed of warrior ready to answer our Nation's call. A common man with uncommon desire to succeed. Forged by adversity, he stands alongside America's finest special operations forces to serve his country, the American people, and protect their way of life. I am that man.
>
> My Trident is a symbol of honor and heritage. Bestowed upon me by the heroes that have gone before, it embodies the trust of those I have sworn to protect. By wearing the Trident, I accept the responsibility of my chosen profession and way of life. It is a privilege that I must earn every day. My loyalty to Country and Team is beyond reproach. I humbly serve as a guardian to my fellow Americans always ready to defend those who are unable to defend themselves. I do not advertise the nature of my work, nor seek recognition for my actions. I voluntarily accept the inherent hazards of my profession, placing the welfare and security of others before my own. I serve with honor on and off the battlefield. The ability to control my emotions and my

---

[1] From the Navy Seals Website http://www.sealswcc.com/navy-seals-ethos.html#.VpM_7sB94y4

actions, regardless of circumstance, sets me apart from other men. Uncompromising integrity is my standard. My character and honor are steadfast. My word is my bond.

We expect to lead and be led. In the absence of orders, I will take charge, lead my teammates and accomplish the mission. I lead by example in all situations. I will never quit. I persevere and thrive on adversity. My Nation expects me to be physically harder and mentally stronger than my enemies. If knocked down, I will get back up, every time. I will draw on every remaining ounce of strength to protect my teammates and to accomplish our mission. I am never out of the fight.

We demand discipline. We expect innovation. The lives of my teammates and the success of our mission depend on me – my technical skill, tactical proficiency, and attention to detail. My training is never complete. We train for war and fight to win. I stand ready to bring the full spectrum of combat power to bear in order to achieve my mission and the goals established by my country. The execution of my duties will be swift and violent when required yet guided by the very principles that I serve to defend. Brave men have fought and died building the proud tradition and feared reputation that I am bound to uphold. In the worst of conditions, the legacy of my teammates steadies my resolve and silently guides my every deed. I will not fail."

ULTIMATE WARRIORS

Just by reading the Navy SEALs' official ethos statement, you can already see just how specialized these men are. In order for someone to live up to such a creed, he needs to be highly intelligent, very fit physically, and must have very good control over himself, particularly his emotions. They are the ultimate of all modern day warriors and as such, only the cream of the crop and the best of the best are able to become official members of this very elite team.

Many people think that there are many, many Navy SEALs in active duty, probably due to the many action movies that portray them as men of steel that are able to overcome almost anything. But the truth is, there are only around 2,000 plus Navy SEALs in active duty. They are that elite.

Such a small number isn't due to lack of men wanting to join the unit. In fact, there are a lot of men who would be willing to do anything if only to become a Navy SEAL. The reason for such a small number is the very stringent qualifications and standards required all who want to become a Navy Seal.

If you think becoming an active member of any United States Special Forces team is hard enough, becoming a Navy SEAL is even harder. This is because Navy SEALs are trained in practically all fields in which all US Special Forces are trained but to an even higher level of competency. To get an idea of just how hard their trainings can be, think about these.

The average training period for successful Navy SEALs applicants lasts for over a year. But in order to be formally accepted into training, you'll need to have vision that's 20/200 at worse that's correctible to 20/20 and pass the unit's very demanding physical screening test.

Just to qualify for formal Navy SEALs training, you'll need to swim at least 500 yards in less than 12:30 and in less than 10:30 if you want to have higher chances of besting out other candidates. You'll need to do at least 42 pushups in 2 minutes and if you want to compete well against the other candidates, you'll need to do at least 79 of them. You'll also have to do at least 50 sit-ups within 2 minutes and if you want to increase your chances of getting in, you need to do at least 79 of them within the same time frame. From a dead hang, you'll have to complete 6 pull-ups with no time limit and complete at least 11 if you want to be competitive with other applicants.

That's not all though. You'll also need to run in just your boots and uniform pants for at least 1.5 miles in less than 11:30 and if you want higher chances of getting in, you'll need to do that in less than 10:20. Only if you're able to pass these physical tests and place higher than most other applicants can you formally begin training as a Navy Seal, which involves land warfare, diving and physical conditioning for 24 weeks and further qualification trainings for 26 weeks more. After more than 50 weeks of training, you'll also have to undergo further specialization trainings such as dynamic entry, surreptitious entry, jumpmaster, diving, rope climbing, fluency in other languages and sniping.

Considering the very few of the multitudes who pass the qualification tests for formal training, you'd understand why there are only quite a handful of Navy SEALs on active duty.

- I will never quit
- I persevere and thrive on adversity
- I am never out of the fight
- I will not fail
- I WILL NEVER RING THE BELL.

The training itself is so difficult that many who enter do not complete it. It's estimated that only up to 35% of those who qualified for formal training ever finish the whole training program, also known as the Basic Underwater Demolition training or BUD training, and become full-fledged members of the United States Navy SEALs. The Trident pin is given to successful recruits upon successful completion of the training program, which symbolizes their official status as a Navy SEAL.

The very purpose of such an agonizing training program is not only to create SEALs, but to ensure that each new SEAL is the best they can be. There is but one standard all members adhere to: unparalleled expertise in the art of war. Each and every one of them must be the very top of the line. The only thing that may set individual SEALs apart is rank and combat experience. When it comes to mastering the training and the doctrine, nothing short of perfection is tolerated.

With over 200 claimed, and around 160 confirmed combat kills over four tours in Iraq, Chief Chris Kyle is the epitome of what a trained Navy SEAL and his weapon can accomplish. As I'm sure we all know by now, this particular SEAL has earned himself a place among legends as the most prolific military sniper in American history.

What's also fascinating is that judging by his subsequent book and other accounts of his story, he wasn't even aware of just how effective he was at his duty. Others later informed him that the military has credited him as being the most lethal marksman in the history of US armed forces. This just goes to show that it's not a reach for glory or recognition; it is just how effective and well trained these men are, the results come naturally. Chris Kyle, in his own words, was merely doing his job, preventing the enemy from harming his fellow US troops. His training and specialization ran their course, and it turns out the results were groundbreaking.

Regardless of how you may feel about this feat, it is undeniable that such a result lies far beyond the capabilities of ordinary men, and no matter how predisposed one may be, it is only through very special training that accomplishments like this are made possible.

One can be a talented shooter, what we call a natural, born leader, or he can have the genetic predisposition towards physical strength. He can have some innate tools within him, yes, but these must be sharpened and honed perfectly if their full potential is to be achieved. As the process of building a

Navy SEAL begins through training, those who have what it takes are gradually filtered through the selections and only then do they begin to assume the final form carved out by the rigorous program. This isn't to say that only those with a "gift" can make it as SEALs, more often than not, determination and perseverance can more than compensate for any initial shortcomings.

NOT JUST PHYSICAL, IT'S ALSO MENTAL

The Navy SEALs training program isn't just a very physically demanding one. It's also very challenging mentally. The mental aspect of such training is what breaks most candidates into quitting.

For example, if you're already in a relatively hypothermic state, think violent chills; will you quickly follow your trainer if he tells you to go back into the water? However insane or inhuman such trainings can be, they are needed in order to produce men who are capable of pulling off very critical and high risk missions such as that of raiding Osama Bin Laden's compound, where during that mission, one of the two helicopters that carried the Navy SEALs operatives crashed inside the compound. When that happened, the operatives of that mission needed to keep their wits in order to finish the mission, or at the very least stay alive. Considering that it happened in one of the deadliest places on earth, panicking is tantamount to death – and a potentially very painful one at that. There are many other examples of the SEALS' valor and perseverance throughout their operational history. When the going gets tough, or even completely out of hand, these guys are still able to adapt and surmount any complications. Preparation is half the battle; the other half is presuming the unexpected. The nature of war is such that anything can go wrong at any moment, despite all the planning and intelligence.

One such instance occurred during the US invasion of Grenada in 1983. A detachment of the Navy SEAL Team Six was tasked with dropping in just off the coast and proceeding ashore via boats air-dropped along with them. Spread out between two cargo planes, the eight SEALs soon found themselves in a string of unfortunate events. Namely, one of the two planes deviating off-course, coupled with adverse weather conditions, ultimately led to four SEALs being lost to the sea. Nonetheless, the remainder of the operatives carried on with their objectives despite the calamity that hindered their insertion.

Evidently, even when disaster strikes, a special breed of men that are the Navy SEALS will overcome the odds stacked against them and see their mission through. The primary factor in making the SEALs what they are is, indeed, the training.

HELL WEEK

A crucial part, the make or break one, of candidates' training is the Hell Week named appropriately because it is a figurative hell on earth for most mortals. Hell week is conducted around the 3rd week of candidates' First Phase training and just before the United States Navy decides to invest heavily and expensively in the candidates in terms of SEAL operations trainings.

This week requires candidates to spend under 6 days in intensely difficult, wet and cold training conditions and run 200 miles on less than four hours of sleep. It's specifically designed that way in order to assess the candidates' ability to perform under extremely high mental and physical stress and sleep-deprived states as well as their attitudes, ability to work with a team, tolerance for cold and pain, mental toughness, and physical endurance. Most of all, Hell Week tests the candidates' most defining characteristics: desire and determination.

It is standard practice to have the candidates sitting or lying down in the very cold Pacific waters while tied together, arm in arm. Conducting physical exercises while exposed to oncoming waves as well as being covered in mud are also part of the torture. All of these excruciating ordeals are inflicted upon all of the candidates at the same time; they have to take it as a team. From the very first phase of training, the prospective SEALs are barraged by torment after torment, giving them a taste of things to come and strengthening or breaking their resolve. More so than just weeding out undetermined and unfit candidates, this process starts developing a sense of camaraderie and team effort from the very beginning. This is how unbreakable bonds are formed between teammates. After they have graduated, the SEALs will walk, eat, breathe and live as one and for each other. In fact, this kind of bond formation is rooted in our very nature. Humans have evolved to develop these connections in times of crisis and anguish, increasing the chances of survival for the whole collective, and thus, each individual member as well. It's a simple mechanism and no phenomenon really; the odds of coming through victorious greatly increase when people come together and focus on a collective goal.

To get an idea how "hellish" Hell Week can be, consider its attrition rate. Only about one-quarter of the few candidates who qualified for BUD successfully finish it. Those who do, consider being an official Navy SEAL to be the single biggest achievement of their lives and come to discover that they can do exceedingly more than what they ever thought was humanly possible. Under the most severe and dangerous mission conditions, they look back to the moment that they successfully finished Hell Week and know that failure isn't an option. It empowers them to never let a teammate down or quit the fight. Indeed, Hell Week is the ultimate test of a man's character, resiliency, and ability to get things done.

Just to give you an idea of the kinds of exercises trainees do during hell week, consider the sugar cookie. The recruits perform the sugar cookie by getting into the very cold waters of the Pacific Ocean after which they roll over and over again in the sand. And just when they start to feel warm enough, they are told to go back into the very cold water and do it again. If you think that is already hard considered the fact that they do it while tired and hungry.

It's interesting to note that men who have experiences in boxing, wrestling, swimming, rugby, lacrosse, triathlons and water polo tend to successfully complete the SEALs training program, according to published article in a San Diego newspaper called the North County Times. If there's any sound basis for the report, it's probably the demanding nature of those disciplines that helped prepare them well for BUD.

CHAPTER 2: NAVY SEALS TRAINING

I'm sure that at this point, you're very intrigued with the particulars of the trainings Navy SEALs recruits go through. After making the cut by finishing the basic boot camp, candidates undergo a seven to nine week pre-BUD apprenticeship-training program. The purpose of the pre-BUD training is to make sure that candidates are adequately prepared for the very physical nature of BUDS training.

The Navy SEAL's candidates training program is one that can stress any man beyond their limits and because of this, candidates are prepared to ensure they successfully complete it and effectively augment the relatively few number of what's probably the world's most elite fighting unit. Candidates need to focus, prepare, and understand what they're getting into.

The Navy SEALs training program helps prepare candidates for the actual and very extreme mental and physical challenges of the typical Navy SEALs missions. If the candidates are up for the challenge, they inevitably get into phenomenal physical shape and conditioning as well as acquire great determination, skills, and confidence that are needed in order to succeed in modern combat or fighting environments.

In the following section, we will look at the training phases that a candidate must undergo if he is to officially become a Navy SEAL. As is obvious, all SEALs must undergo the BUD/S training – but their work starts even before they join the Basic Underwater Demolition/SEAL. Training at BUD/S goes for almost 24 weeks, following which they will be asked to learn further skills like basic parachuting. At the end of this time period, they must take the 26 week SEAL Qualification Training Program.

All those soldiers who join the SEAL training who also have medical training or knowledge have attended another 6 month Advanced Medical Training Course so that they can become part of the Medic Units. And even after completion of BUD/S training and certification as a SEAL, even after they have been given a spot on a SEAL team, they are not done – they can expect up to 18 months of training on the job, though they will have leave in between to rest and recuperate.

Before we even look at what the training entails, let us check out some quick statistical data. This should tell you just how hard it is to complete a SEAL Training program and why these men are so strong, both physically and mentally.

Of all the numbers who signed up to join the SEALs, around 85 - 90% of them complete the pre-BUDS indoctrination tests. These are relatively easier to complete, as we will see soon. BUD/S is the proverbial nightmare for you and I – it is the most difficult part of the SEAL training and very few people who sign up manage to complete the whole course and get themselves certified as SEALs. Research shows that only around 33% of the total recruits finish Phase 1 of the training program and even fewer manage to make it to second and third phases and then graduate.

The prerequisites to join the SEALs are very simple. A person must be at least 18 years of age, usually between the age gap of 18 to 29 years old, who are citizens of the United States of America and are part of the U.S. Navy. Of course, there have been a number of instances when military personnel from armed forces belonging to other countries that are allies of the United States also take part in BUDS training. If the parents are willing to permit it, waivers are available for the 17 year olds who are interested – they are also given to 30 year olds, depending on their individual circumstance and situation.

When it comes to academics, it is expected that all prospective applicants must be at least as qualified as a high school student with a diploma or a GED. They must also have a composite score a minimum of 220 on the ASVAB test. If you don't know what that is – ASVAB is the Armed Services Vocational Aptitude Battery Test, a multiple options paper that the United States Military Entrance Processing Command administers in grades 10, 11 and 12 of high school to identify those interested and qualified to enlist as part of the military. Students who want to enlist for the SEALs must be proficient in every aspect of the English language.

When it comes to physical fitness, things get even trickier. All the prospective SEAL students must have a vision that at least 20/75, which can be corrected to a 20/20 vision once they begin training. They must not have a recent history of drug abuse and every prospective applicant is required the take a SEAL Physical Screening Test to make sure that they will be able to keep up with the harsh requirements of the physical training regimen that the BUDS offer. Finally, the applicant must be a person with a good and moralistic character, as evidenced by his history of criminal records and even his civil citations.

As of August in the year 2015, there has been talk of women finally joining the Navy SEALs! It is the last and only regiment of the entire United States military that has not been opened to the female sex. The bill has been passed; however, actually getting things into motion is going to be far more difficult. The military stands firm on the idea that the standards should not be lowered for women – they must be able to meet the same physical requirements as their male counterparts. While this may sound unfair to you, it is for good reason. Given the handful of soldiers who pass the BUDS Program as it is, if standards were lowered, the resultant soldiers would not be as tough or powerful as they end up being currently. It is not an easy task, but it can be done – we may soon see a female SEAL!

NAVY SEAL PHYSICAL SCREENING TEST (PST)

So how does the BUD/S Training Program work? If you want to sign up to be a Navy SEAL, you must train for your training! You have to be physically fit enough to qualify and make sure your academic score is at least good, if not exceptional. As we saw earlier, to join the BUD/S Training Program, a person must pass the SEAL Physical Screening Test, or the PST. Now, the minimum requirements for this test are easy enough for those who are relatively physically fit. They are –

- A five hundred yard (460 m) swim, wherein you make use of the breaststroke or the combat stroke. Your competitive time must be at 9 minutes, preferably lesser than that.
- A minimum of 50 pushups in under 2 minutes, though the competitive count set is epxe4cted to be at least 90 or more than that.
- A minimum of 50 sit ups in under 2 minutes, though the competitive count set is once again expected to be at least 90 or more than that.
- A minimum of at least 10 pull ups from a dead hang weight, and though there is no time limit on this, the competitive count is expected to be at least 18 or more than that.
- Run for 1.5 miles (2.4 km), wearing running shorts and boots, in less than 10.30 minutes, though, again, your competitive time is expected to be 9.30 minutes or less.

As you can see for yourself, prospective SEAL candidates cannot just meet minimum requirements – they have to be much, *much* better than the minimum requirements to be even considered to be part of the SEALs. This means that anyone who is considering joining the SEALs must do enough preparatory work and get themselves into a physically fit status quo that will allow them to clear the PST.

The minimum is there only to formally set the bar somewhere, but it goes without saying that a candidate must strive to far surpass it, if he is hoping to compete for his place in this select group of warriors. Keep in mind that there will be some very tough guys applying at the same time so all candidates must give it their absolutely best shot. This means that it's not about fulfilling a minimum requirement, or "passing the test," it is about truly distinguishing yourself and shining compared to your peers. As you can see, even the selection process in the Navy SEALs already begins separating the very best from the rest.

NAVAL SPECIAL WARFARE PREPARATORY SCHOOL

When you pass the first physical screen test, you are put into preparatory school for the BUDS Training Program. That's right – you prepare before your PST to go to preparatory school. That is how difficult getting into the SEALs is.

The Naval Special Warfare Preparatory School is currently located in Great Lakes, Illinois. This is where your training for the Basic Underwater Demolition/SEAL begins; the prospective candidates are given a crash course in BUDS to show them what they are in for if they do move into the program. To get into the program itself, they must go through a second Physical Screening Test at the end of this preparatory school.

Here, the candidates undergo this physically challenging training for a period of 8 weeks. At the end this time period, the second Physical Screening Test that I mentioned is administered to them – a timed 4 mile run, along with a 1000 meter swim is included in this test. As with the previous screening, just meeting minimum requirements does not guarantee entry into the SEALs – you must go above and beyond and do exceptionally well to be inducted into the BUDS Training School.

While this may seem extensive to you – training to get into training to get into more training – it is absolutely essential to prepare the candidates. As we will further see, the BUD/S Training is the most difficult and physically challenging regimen that any military team has to offer. It requires grit, determination and physical fitness levels that very few people possess, which means that it is obviously not easy to complete. Those who do not pass their second physical screening are not kicked out of the Navy – they are simply not given admission into the SEAL training pipeline. Instead, they are reclassified and sent to other jobs and posts within the Navy itself.

With all its horrors, the entirety of the Navy SEAL training pays for itself and shows the best result in the end. After all, the SEALs have a reputation to keep, and that reputation is of a unit that is few in numbers but is so elite that their name rings out loudly and proudly throughout the US armed forces as well as the rest of the world. As a matter of fact, Navy SEALs are a source of inspiration for many similar forces in the modern world. They are a unit that sets new standards and maintains the old ones. The SEALs have also trained with many forces, which aspire towards their level of professionalism.

So you can see what is at stake, and you now know why there is so much training before the actual training even begins. When the candidates have made all the cuts, they are ready to embark upon the ultimate feat and get on their way to attaining the revered Trident insignia.

And then begins BUD/S.

BUD/S (BASIC UNDERWATER DEMOLITION/SEALS) TRAINING PROGRAM

The Basic Underwater Demolition/SEAL Training program is geared towards developing both the physical as well as the mental fitness of all the candidates who sign up to be Navy SEALs. It focuses on their leadership skills, their physical fitness, their emotional fitness and their mental toughness by putting them through different phases of training. This is a seven-month long training program that's designed to develop the recruits or candidates' physical and mental stamina as well as their leadership skills. Every phase of the BUDS training program includes physical conditioning tests with increasingly demanding time requirements every week. And as mentioned earlier, candidates need to pass the following physical screening test requirements in order to get into the program:

- Swim at least 500 yards within 12:30 at most;
- Perform at least 42 pushups in 2 minutes;
- Do at least 50 sit-ups within 2 minutes;
- Perform at least 6 pull-ups from a dead hanging position (no time limit); and
- Run 1.5 miles wearing only their boots and uniform pants within 11:30.

The first step in a SEALs training is the Indoctrination into the BUDS program – this step lasts for a total of three weeks. Following this, there are three major phases of training for the SEALs to complete. The first phase, which lasts for seven weeks, is focused on getting the candidates physically fit by putting them through the most difficult and challenging physical situations possible.

The second phase, once again lasting for a period of seven weeks, is geared towards underwater combat, particularly combat diving and it is followed by the final seven week period of the third phase, which is directed towards teaching the men how to perform land warfare. Whether one is an enlisted soldier or an officer, there is no difference in treatment – all personnel go through the same training program and are expected to give it their best shot, regardless of experience or standing in the military. The point of the program, after all, is to test mental strength, and build a sense of teamwork and camaraderie, so everyone is put through the same mental and physical training. Let us take a look at each phase of BUD/S training one by one.

STAGE 1 – INDOCTRINATION (INDOC) – 3 WEEKS

The Indoctrination Phase provides the candidates with an introduction to the BUDS training program's technique and performance requirements. This is the first stage in the BUD/S Training Program for the Navy SEALs. It is the initiation phase, so to speak, that is conducted over the course of three weeks, once the candidates complete their 8-week training regimen at the Naval Special Warfare Preparatory School in Illinois.

The idea of this stage in BUD/S is to introduce the prospective SEALs to the kind of life they can expect during their training. The Navy SEAL instructors will introduce the men to the BUD/S physical training, particularly the obstacle course, and also give them a crash course on all the other training practices that are unique to the Navy SEAL lifestyle. Candidates are prepared to start their first phase of BUD/S training, which follows immediately after this one.

As you can probably guess, this phase, even though it's light, is the true beginning of BUD/S training and is quite challenging. The prospective SEALs meet their instructors, get to know exactly what it is they will be doing over the course of the next few months and then learn to adapt themselves to it. This is also the time when they begin to meet their fellow SEALs trainees and make friends – a sense of camaraderie begins right from this initiation point that will continue all the way on to the battlefield after they graduate. The bond formed between men who have been through the hell of Navy SEAL training together is a truly unbreakable and everlasting force. This relationship carries them a long-way through combat missions and is one of the most important factors in building an elite and effective military unit. The friendship and loyalty are only strengthened through potential combat and usually stay for life. An individual SEAL is a formidable force on his own, but it's only when he is part of the collective entity of his unit that all the training begins to truly kick in and make SEALs stand out among the rest.

STAGE 2 – THREE PHASES OF BUD/S TRAINING

Phase 1 – Physical Conditioning – 7 weeks

The First Phase, also known as the basic conditioning phase, is the hardest of all three phases in the BUDS training program. It lasts for seven weeks and peaks at the halfway point with Hell Week. It's at that point where the candidates' physical and mental limits will be most tested. For those who persist until the end, even while their bodies scream and beg for them to just drop the whole thing, the sweetest words they'll ever hear are the instructor's "Hell Week is secured!"

This first phase covers a variety of things that are essential for a SEAL's lifestyle on the field – they are taught to keep their bodies fit, how to turn themselves into a weapon, how to work under the water, how to work and be part of a team, how to challenge themselves and their own limits constantly to build mental toughness and strength. Physically conditioning is the hardest in this phase – it is used as a method to build mental toughness and tenacity. Running for miles together without rest or resources, swimming in all kinds of untoward conditions, heavy duty calisthenics, harsh obstacle courses and the like are administered one by one, with the difficulty level increasing each week.

As we said earlier on, the most important and difficult part of the program is the Hell Week. This is the third week during the seven-week rotation and the first two weeks of the first phase in BUD/S are geared towards preparing the candidates for this strenuous time. During Hell Week, the prospective SEALs are put through grueling physical exercises.

For five and a half continuous days, they are expected to train with little to no rest. Data suggests that each candidate gets maybe four hours of sleep over the course of the entire week – they are expected to run for long distances, easily about two hundred miles or so, and their physical training lasts close to 20 hours or so in a single day. You can see why it is called the Hell Week – one literally goes through a grueling physical hell. Just try to envision going through such physical strain with next to no sleep and limited food intake. Even the very lines of reality can become blurred in this state, which is why this process isolates only the primal, most brute force and dedication in a human being. A candidate's basic, even animalistic, instincts and energy will be harnessed to their full potential during this trial of wits and strength, ultimately molding them into the finest, most perfected fighting machine humanity has to offer. These facts don't serve merely to illustrate how horrendous the BUD/S training is, but they are also foreshadowing of the kinds of circumstances these soldiers may find themselves in over the course of their careers.

And this is where the concept of mental toughness comes in. If one is not determined to complete the training, if one is mentally not strong enough to push oneself into finishing it, one will have no choice but to drop out. The SEALs use this type of extensive physical workouts and grueling physical sessions to teach their men how to be strong – they are, literally, taught to use their bodies to tame their minds. Pain is a tool for them, and as romantic as it sounds, it is not – it's probably both the best and the worst experience of their lives. As Kevin Lacz, a former Navy SEAL and comrade of late Chris Kyle, has been recorded saying for the Fox News: "It's the most fun you never wanna have again."

Once Hell Week ends, the strain of the physical conditioning peters off the slightest bit – they have been put through the worst kind of challenge, and so, they are granted the smallest reprieve. That doesn't mean that they are off the hook though! The rest of the first phase training period is usually spent on teaching the candidates how to conduct hydrographic surveys. Since SEALs are closely involved in the Naval Operations, they need to be familiar with maritime warfare and navigation, which is what they are taught. They are taught to use aircrafts, electronic sensor systems and the like to learn how to navigate the ocean and become better warriors of both stealth and power.

As should be obvious by now, given the challenge that is the first phase, a large number of candidates question their ability to complete the BUD/S training program itself. A significant drop in numbers usually happens at this stage – it is to be expected, given how difficult it is and just how much is expected out of them. The military does not penalize them for it; there is the Drop on Request (DOR) option offered to them that they could avail of if they find it too much. The tradition of the DOR is that the candidate drops his helmet liner next to the pole, which has a ship's bell, attached to it. After dropping his helmet, the candidate rings the bell three times, indicating that he is done and he cannot take much more.

This ensures that only the toughest and strongest men get through the SEAL training – they are the ones entrusted with the most challenging of missions, ones whose outcomes could mean millions of lives. There is no judgment on those who cannot complete the first phase or Hell Week; the military accepts them as part of other branches to which their talents are well suited. But the SEALs must be the toughest and most powerful of the lot, given that they are to be the elite team of fighters, first in line to defend their country.

So, to sum up, the First Phase includes the following activities during its 7-week duration the following activities that become harder and harder as the weeks progress:

- Sand running;
- Ocean swims for 2 miles with fins;
- Calisthenics;

- Timed obstacle courses;
- Timed runs in boots for 4 miles;
- Basic seamanship with small boats;
- Creating charts and hydrographic surveys;
- Hell Week at week 3, which is 5 ½ days of non-stop training (including the "sugar cookie", swimming, running and enduring exhaustion, wet and cold conditions with only a total of 4 hours of sleep);
- Rock Portage in Rubber Raiding Craft;

I don't need to tell you that by the end of Hell Week, most of them are heavily exhausted and/or injured. All candidates, therefore, are put through two medical examinations to ensure their safety within twenty-four hours after they complete Hell Week. This is to keep them physically fit, as well as to encourage them by showing them that what they are doing is not in vain – fight for the country and the country will fight back for you.

Phase 2 – Combat Diving – 7 weeks

The second phase of BUD/S begins soon after the first ends and lasts for a period of seven weeks once again. So far, in the first phase, candidates were set towards building up their physical fitness and condition themselves to adapt to the toughest and most challenging situations. Now, a transition is made from land to water – the second phase focuses on getting the candidates to be competent combat swimmers.

As you can guess, the physical training that they are continued to be put through becomes even more rigorous, with added element of water fitness being thrown in. candidates who are not comfortable in water or have a fear of water will definitely fail this phase; from diving to swimming, every candidate is expected to undergo combat instruction without complaint.

The focus in on training them to be better swimmers as well as combat scuba divers. There are two types of SCUBA diving that the candidates are put through – open circuit scuba diving with compressed air and then closed circuit scuba diving. For those who do not know the difference, the open circuit diving involves using a breather that has only compressed air, whereas the closed circuit diving breather continues 100% pure oxygen instead of just plain compressed air. Both are not exactly easy to master and the candidates have to extremely fit to master these techniques.

Apart from combat diving, the prospective SEALs are also taught how to take care of themselves under the water – basic dive medicine courses are administered, as are detailed medical skills that they will find useful in the field.

What separates the SEALs from other United States Special Forces is their ability to make use of swimming and diving techniques as a means of transport. This means that there is special focus given to underwater dives on a longer distance – not only do they have to be good combat divers, they must be able to withstand the pressures of the ocean for as long a distance as is possible for them. This way, their diving techniques become extremely valuable, especially when they can transport them from the launch point to their objective, which few of the other military forces are capable of doing.

It goes without saying that only the candidates who are good with water complete this phase successfully. As difficult as the first phase of training was, with Hell Week and grueling physical training, the second is even more challenging. The environment becomes even more hostile than previously – they must navigate treacherous waters, often times at extreme temperatures and execute complex maneuvers in stressful situations.

Once again, the SEALs try to further build mental toughness by allowing their students to experience extreme physical challenges. Only the toughest men can get through to the third phase, which begins soon after this one ends.

So to sum it up, only the select few who survived the attrition that's the first phase proceed to Phase 2, also known as the diving phase, which lasts for yet another seven weeks and includes:

-Higher intensity physical training;

-Combat diving skills;

-Scuba diving with compressed air, a.k.a., open circuit scuba diving;

-Scuba diving with 100% oxygen, a.k.a., closed-circuit scuba diving;

-Extended-distance underwater diving; and

-Mission-specific combat diving and swimming techniques.

This type of training lets them become comfortable with all kinds of physical environments and they learn to adapt themselves to their situation.

Phase 3 – Land Warfare – 7 weeks

The third and final phase of the BUD/S Training Program also goes for a period of seven weeks, during which the recruits learn to actually fight and how to act in a war. From the under the water combat diving tactics, the focus shifts back on to land, this time focusing on training with actual weapons.

The prospective SEAL candidates are taught how to handle basic, classic weapons, how to use and make demolitions out of the limited resources they have around them within the immediate vicinity, how to navigate the terrain despite not being familiar with it, how to patrol and rappel down rocks and walls, how to shoot long distances and overall, how to turn themselves and their own bodies into dangerous weapons. There is emphasis placed on how to use strategy for small units; given that most SEAL missions take place in secret, with each unit being tightly knit and sent into the field together, you can understand how this might be an important lesson to learn.

Unlike the first and the second phases of training, the third is more classroom oriented than physical. The idea is to teach the students how to gather information and data that is required to complete the mission, process this data and then react, as the situation demands it. Skills such as how to read and make basic maps, how to use the stars and the compass to navigate unknown territory, using innocuous objects as survival tools, etc., are given a lot of importance and the recruits are prepared for actual missions out in the field.

You could say that the first and the second phases of training were conditioning of the body and the mind while the third is the actual prep work required to be out in the field on actual, real life missions. They candidates go from being mere novices to full functioning SEALs and soldiers who can survive under any and all conditions.

To further drive this point home, the candidates are taken on an actual onsite simulation. The last three and a half weeks of the third phase, the team is transported to San Clemente Island, which is located around 60 miles from Coronado, where they are required to put into practice all the skills that they have learnt so far. The days are long and they are expected to survive out in the harsh conditions, each day mirroring and simulating the circumstances of an actual mission and being in the field.

Once again, this becomes a repetition of Hell Week in a manner of speaking – there is very little sleep that they can afford and training happens dawn to dusk, seven days in a week. To make matters worse, they also are expected to work with live explosives, demolitions and ammunition. Every aspect of it is similar to actually being out in the field – this is to prepare them for the reality they will face when they are on missions. A lot of candidates fail in this round because the instructors – who are in charge of making sure they have the skills they need to survive warfront – are extremely strict and dole out the harshest punishments yet.

So, finally – the Third and final phase – Land Warfare – is where the candidates undergo training for handling weapons and military land and underwater explosives, rappelling, tactical small units operations and navigating different land terrains, among others for seven weeks. It includes:

- More strenuous physical conditioning;
- Weapons handling;
- Use of explosives;
- Small unit combat tactics and strategies;
- Patrolling;
- Rappelling and other rope operations; and
- Sniping or marksmanship.

With this, the final phase of BUD/S training comes to an end. Remember the importance of the mental aspect of SEALs training? Most candidates who failed the BUDS program did so not because of the physical issues but because of either academics or safety and competency issues, both of which require optimal mental performance.

After BUDS, the focus of the candidates' trainings shifts from testing for their high-stress environment behaviors, reactions and instincts to building their core competencies.

POST BUDS TRAINING

Right after successfully completing BUDS, the candidates immediately proceed to a three-week training on the basics of parachuting. After which, the candidates go through a final qualification training program for eight weeks, which focuses on procedures, techniques, tactics, operations and missions planning.

Being well versed in different aspects of modern warfare, even if they don't necessarily relate to naval operations, is crucial in making the SEALs a versatile unit. Thanks to their all-encompassing specialization, they are able to answer the call and excel in all manner of operations, be it on American soil or abroad.

Parachute Jump School – 3 Weeks

Once the three challenging phases of their BUD/S Training Program is over, the prospective SEAL candidates are given basic knowledge on how to parachute. This training is geared towards making them able parachuters, both in static and free falling parachute types.

The candidates ate taken to Tactical Air Operations in San Diego, where the program is administered. The program lasts over a period of three weeks and it has been designed such that the participants learn how to become competent free fall jumpers within the shortest time possible. It is a highly accelerated program, which has some of the best instructors in the world – they are focused on making sure that the SEALs turn out to be the best jumpers they can be in the little time given to them.

In order to finish the course, the SEALs candidates must go through a series of jump progressions. These range from basic static line falls to accelerated free falls and includes even making use of combat equipment. The ultimate goal is finish a night descent while carrying combat equipment, from a height of at least 9500 feet. As you can guess, this is no easy task – men with a fear of heights will find it extremely difficult. But, as SEALs do, they will overcome this fear and master the jump. After surviving Hell Week, the men will already be operating on a whole new level of dedication as the final goal comes increasingly close to their grasp. As a matter of fact, according to a Navy Times report published a few years back, the graduation rate in SEAL airborne school is 100%. This rate is undoubtedly due to the fact that their parachute course comes after the BUD/S training, which means that those who weren't cut out for it have already dropped the ball. After BUD/S, making a few parachute jumps is far from enough to make those who have come so close give up. By this time, the candidates will have learned to master any irrational and baseless fears they may have, and parachuting is definitely one of those since it is completely safe, technically.

GRADUATION

The Navy SEALs candidates' training concludes with the BUDS class graduation, where the very few and proud dress in their Navy uniforms.

Then they get the highly coveted symbol of being official Navy SEALs, the Trident insignia or pin that they wear on their uniforms.

Their achievements are recognized in the presence of senior SEAL leaders, senior enlisted advisors of Naval Special Warfare groups, naval commanding officers, other SEALs teams, and family members. During the graduation, and successful candidates are reminded of just how special the group that they're formally joining is and for them to be worthy of the sacrificial acts of those who courageously went before them.

SEAL TRAINING AFTER GRADUATION

Like I mentioned earlier on, training for the Navy SEALs does not end with just qualification into the SEAL program or becoming part of the SEALs. Even after they graduate, they are put through extensive training before they are sent out on missions. If you think about it, the BUD/S, though the most difficult program on earth to pass, is really only a blip on the radar when it comes to actual experience or skills required to face down terrorists and insurgents and all other dangers. No wonder, then, that the military puts them through even more rigorous training regimens after they become SEALs officially.

Seal Troop Training

Once they have been assigned to a SEAL Team/Troop and placed with a subordinate platoon, they are given more training to get them battle ready. This pre-deployment workup can last anywhere between 12 t 18 months and is once again divided into three phases – individuality specialty training, unit level training and task group level training.

Individuality Specialty Training

As the name suggests, the training is to develop specialized skills among the platoon members to designate them to a particular position within the team. The individuality specialty training usually last for a period of about 6 months and the individual candidates attend a number of courses. These courses are designed to teach them necessary skills that will make the whole platoon an operational combat team, depending on where they are needed and what they are required to do. Here are a few of the skills that are focused on extensively –

- Sniping
- Scouting
- Close Quarter Combat
- Barrier Penetration and Methods of Entry, including Surreptitious Entry
- Technical Surveillance Operations
- Driving Skills, including defensive driving, rally driving and protective security
- Climbing
- Parachute Rigging and Jumping
- Diving
- Advanced Demolition
- High Threat Protective Security
- Language School

There are many, many more skills, each of which are taught to specific team members depending on which platoon they are serving in and what is required of them.

Unit Level Training

As the name suggests, this is the second phase of SEAL training where the focus is on the unit as a whole. Again lasting usually for a period of about six months, Unit Level Training is geared towards improving their core mission skills such as –

- Land warfare
- Urban warfare

- Close quarter combat
- Combat swimming
- Long range target interdiction
- Rotary as well as fixed wing air operations
- Reconnaissance

The focus is on developing the unit as a whole – teamwork is given utmost importance as is using individual skills to make the entire platoon a success.

Task Group Level Training

Once again lasting for a period of about 6 months or so, the final phase in SEAL training is the Task Group Level Training. The group undergoes advanced training with supporting attachments of a SEAL Squadron such as the Special Boat Teams, the Intelligence Teams, the Cryptological Support Teams, the Medical Teams, the Communication Teams, and the like. This is to familiarize them with all the resources the military has to offer them and teach them to learn to work in symbiosis with the whole military, beyond just their platoon alone.

As you can see, the training is geared to developing both individual skills as well making them a part of a whole – first of the SEAL platoon, and then of the entire Navy and the military itself. SEALs have a drawn out sense of team spirit and brotherhood for a reason; out there, in the field, if you can't depend on your comrade, you may as well throw in the towel.

With this, the final phase of SEAL training is completed. They are officially considered to be part of the Navy SEALs and deemed ready to go on missions for their country.

Without my pointing it out, it should be obvious by now that the amount of challenges the SEALs face is enormous. They are the toughest, strongest and most capable men on earth – for good reason! They are put through the most grueling of physical training, which amounts to emotional and mental torture for civilians. It teaches them to toughen up and learn to adapt to situations so that they are able to not only survive, but also carry out their mission successfully. You and I cannot possibly undergo such painful training so easily, but we can emulate some of their practices in our own lives to make us stronger people, able to face down any difficult situation without much difficulty.

CHAPTER 3: WHY SHOULD YOU TRAIN LIKE A NAVY SEAL?

The reason is simple: because training like a Navy SEAL will give you the self-confidence you need to succeed in life. When you're as physically and mentally fit and strong as they are, there's no reason for you to feel inferior and incapable of achieving great things. You don't need to be a Navy SEAL to win in life but using the same principles and techniques they do can certainly help you prepare to enjoy great successes in life.

Once you really get to the grass roots of our problems and failures in life, you'll find that most of them are resulting from a simple lack of confidence. Getting that job you want, going for a promotion, taking a step forward in virtually any direction in all walks of life, all of these undertakings require confidence to get things rolling on the right track. Often we may find ourselves not living up to our potential and accomplishing our goals even if we are capable and skilled enough, only because we may be afraid to take action.

Of course, vanity and misguided complacency won't get you anywhere either. What confidence is about is knowing and understanding one's self fully, being aware of our flaws, but working with what we are to the best of our ability and achieving the maximum result. Confidence is not letting your few shortcomings get in the way of your success as you harness your virtues and advantages to their full potential.

PHYSICAL FITNESS

Let's face it, being fit and in shape goes a long way to boost any person's confidence. It may sound rather vain or superficial but that's the truth. Training the way Navy SEALs do can definitely help you get in great physical shape and achieve excellent physical fitness and conditioning.

Being in the best shape of your life is not only about looking good or being attractive. Exercise is primarily about health and wellbeing. When your body is healthy, your mind will be as well; this is just the natural order of things with all living creatures. As you improve your physical shape, you will be tremendously rewarded when you achieve the perfect balance between your mental and physical states. This will in turn significantly boost your overall mindset, mood and, ultimately, confidence. As a matter of fact, feeling healthy and being disciplined will make you more confident than your reflection in the mirror ever could.

EMOTIONAL AND MENTAL TOUGHNESS

Most of our battles in life are mental or emotional. The same holds true for Navy SEALs. While it's true that they're some of the world's most physically superior human specimens, their physical conditioning merely gets them in the front porch of this elite club. Most of the time, what gets them in or kicks them out is mental and emotional toughness or the lack of it. Because of this, only the strongest emotionally and mentally actually make it in and stay there. Confidence is a mental and emotional issue. Training for mental and emotional toughness will definitely make you a confident person.

Once the bullets start whizzing around the soldiers, their physical strength is what fuels their fighting and survival. But, it is their perseverance that pushes them to overcome the odds and prevail in battle, coming out on top each time. Even for us mere mortals, a simple fact of life is that no matter how much of a beating your physical body can withstand, it's only your mental resilience that will keep you from keeling over and calling it quits. It matters not what kind of tools you have at your disposal, without the strength of character and rock-solid power of will, you chances of success will plummet drastically.

NUTRITION

Lastly, all the physical, emotional and mental training in the world may not give you the optimum results you want if you don't have enough energy and nutrients to power you through them. That's why proper nutrition is essential to Navy SEALs training and performance. And to the extent you can master your nutrition is the extent you can successfully train your body, mind and emotions, all of which will lead to higher self-esteem.

People will often neglect, or completely overlook, the importance of strategically planning out your diet. More than just the amount you eat, the kind of food you have and the times of day you eat it are paramount. Make no mistake, successful exercise and daily functioning begin and end with a perfectly balanced, well-structured diet. All military forces in the world since ancient times, especially the likes of Navy SEALs, have known full well that a well-fed soldier is an efficient, strong and motivated one.

CHAPTER 4: FITNESS

Because of the very demanding nature of their missions, Navy SEALs need to be in optimal physical shape to be able to successfully carry them out. With all that moving, running and weapons they need to carry as well as the need to effectively defend themselves, Navy SEALs need to be in great cardiovascular shape on top of being nimble, quick and strong. As such, the cornerstones of the Navy SEALs' fitness programs are cardio workout and calisthenics.

Besides the fact that the nature of their missions often requires traversing incredible distances in adverse conditions, individual SEALs must be in tip-top shape in case disaster strikes as well. Despite all the planning and intelligence, unforeseen circumstances will still occur in war. Sometimes, an individual SEAL might get separated from his unit due to casualties or unfavorable weather conditions.

During a 2005 Afghanistan mission, codenamed Operation Red Wings, a reconnaissance team comprised of four SEALs came under an effective and brutal ambush in Kunar Province, which left three of them killed in action. Marcus Luttrell, although wounded, managed to survive and be rescued, while successfully avoiding capture and contact with the enemy with the help of the locals. Despite the disastrous operation, this man kept his head and saw home again, living to tell his tale. It takes a strong and well-forged frame of mind and body to overcome these situations, and exercise surely plays a big part here.

CARDIO

It's not uncommon to hear about how far from shores Navy SEALs often disembark from to stealthily approach enemy territory and successfully conduct their high-stakes, high-profile missions. They swim from such a far distance with weapons and gear on. I don't know about you but I would consider myself to be in relatively great cardiovascular condition given I can finish 10-kilometer runs but for the life of me, I can't even swim 50 meters straight in the pool with nothing but my Speedos on. And when you consider that they swim with gear for relatively far distances in open water, with currents, and then you begin to see just how much cardiovascular conditioning these guys need.

Then you think about how candidates need to run 1.5 miles in under 11:30 in nothing but their uniform pants and in army boots. Yes, not in high tech modern running shoes but in army training boots. And that's just to qualify for training!

Of course, you don't need to be able to swim in open water, 1 kilometer away from shore with weapons. Nor do you need to be able to run 1.5 miles in under 11:30 in nothing but army boots and pants. But if you want to be in great physical shape and conditioning, you'll need to do regular cardio workouts.

Cardio workouts are exercises that increase your heart rate, improve oxygen delivery to the muscles and burn body fat. Typically, cardio workouts employ large muscle groups for a specified period of time. Using large muscle groups, such as the legs, burn more calories and fat.

Naturally, with each new ground you break in your exercises and with each new record you set for yourself, you gradually become sturdier and tougher. The trick is to keep pushing yourself and keep increasing those distances and timing. Considering that you're not going to be humping claymores, guns and rocket launchers, you can still focus on the numbers we mentioned before, and strive to get on the SEAL level. It can certainly be done.

The most practical way to get regular cardio workouts in is by running. All you need is a good pair of running shoes, running shorts, and a good fitting shirt and you're good to go. You can run in the streets, on trails, on a treadmill in the gym or on an oval track. The only limitation really is your mind and occasionally, the weather. Other excellent forms of cardio workouts include biking and swimming, both of which are better than running in the sense that running and biking don't subject your joints to impact forces but are more expensive and less practical as both need special equipment to perform. Even Navy SEALs run for regular cardio and stamina workouts.

Remember that the core values here are discipline and dedication. If you want to reach a high level of physical ability, it will require certain sacrifices and possibly saying goodbye to some of your favorite viands and snacks. More importantly, there can be no skipping out on training sessions. Imagine if a drill instructor ordered a SEAL to get ready for a running course, and the subordinate "doesn't feel like it", or he prefers to stay in and watch a movie with some snacks – just for today. That won't work.

CALISTHENICS

Bodyweight exercises have been a staple in most civilizations' physical fitness regimens for centuries dating back as far as the Greek and Roman empires. Their armies performed calisthenics to get in great fighting shape, just like the Navy SEALs. Further, they didn't have the benefit of modern exercise equipment like barbells, dumbbells and machines for resistance training. All they really had were trees, rocks, and their bodies. Calisthenics are still more than a relevant form of exercise, especially in the military, mostly due to their simple practicality. Using just your God-given body and its mass, you can achieve much better results than you may initially expect.

The beautiful thing about calisthenics is that it doesn't just help build muscles but that it builds just the right amount of it, as well as functional strength. When it comes to fighting, functional strength is what it's all about. The best way for me to differentiate functional from lifting strength is scaling a wall.

In order to scale a tall wall, you'll need to be able to jump high enough to reach the top with both hands and pull yourself up. In terms of jumping, leg strength is obviously important. So based on leg strength alone, who do you think can jump high enough to reach the top of the wall to hang – a 150 pound gymnast who can only squat 100 pounds or a 300 pound bodybuilder with legs the size of tree trunks and can squat 600 pounds? That's right – it's the gymnast. That's the difference between functional and lifting strength.

Now let's look at pulling themselves up on the wall. Who do you think will be able to scale up that wall by pulling himself up: the gymnast who can only pull down 100 pounds on the lat pull down machine or the bodybuilder who can pull down 300 or even 400 pounds? That's right, the gymnast.

Since Navy SEALs train for strength in order to be quick, nimble and powerful in combat and be strong enough to carry weapons and gear, it goes without saying that they need functional strength more than lifting strength. That's why they hardly use resistance training equipment but instead train with different exercises using just their bodyweight.

As you can see, agility, muscle coordination, and grace of movement are the name of the game. Functional strength has a far wider range of application, which is what makes it the shape of choice for these versatile warriors. On the other hand, lifting strength is good for, well, lifting.

Here are some of the best calisthenics exercises for developing functional strength ala-Navy SEALs:

- Chest/Triceps: Regular grip push-ups and diamond grip push-ups.
- Back/Biceps: Wide-grip pull-ups, reverse-grip pull-ups, bodyweight back extensions and deadlifts with a boulder or heavy objects.
- Legs: Bodyweight squats; bodyweight lunges, jumping squats, single leg bodyweight squats, bodyweight calf-raises, box-jumps, bounds and long jumps from a standing position.
- Core Muscles: Sit-ups, crunches, planks, side-planks, leg raises, hanging leg raises, and trunk twists.
- Overall Strength: Burpees.

As a beginner, start by doing this twice to three times a week and gradually increase frequency to four times a week for each muscle group. Make sure there's at least 48 hours of rest for each muscle group prior to working them out again.

If you work out all the muscle groups in one session, you can only workout four times a week in order to give your muscles at least 48 hours of recovery in between sessions. If you do a split body workout, one body part per session, you can work out every day. For example, you could do legs on Monday, chest on Tuesday, back on Wednesday, core muscles on Thursday and total body on Saturday.

Start with 2 sets of 10 repetitions for each exercise and if it's too easy for you, add repetitions or sets accordingly.

Getting to the Navy SEALs' level of training is a gradual process. It could not and should not be achieved over a short period of time. This holds especially true for us average Joes; going at it too intensely and too fast will not produce the desired results and may even leave you injured or otherwise hinder your health. This is why the SEALs make sure that their candidates are regularly checked for any problems as they develop and advance through their training step by step. Be fast to begin training, but take your time as you build up your strength and stamina, this is the best way to get the most out of your exercise.

CHAPTER 5: COURAGE

"Courage is resistance to fear, mastery of fear, not the absence of fear." - Mark Twain

The ability to master one's emotions is crucial for any form of personal success, be it in terms of relationships, career, finances, or just about any endeavor that is worth pursuing. If you want to at least be a good leader, you'll need to inspire your followers or subordinates not with mere words but with courage. Nothing else erodes credibility with and trust of followers and subordinates than showing fear in the midst of challenging situations. At the same time, no factor is as crucial in leadership as the personal example. Not just in military and combat, but in ordinary walks of life, setting an example can motivate subordinates to no limits, and not just subordinates, but peers and even complete strangers. Entire revolutions have been sparked on this principle.

The history of warfare, in particular, is full of such instances. If I may be allowed a slight divergence from our main topic for a minute, I'm going to make mention of a very interesting video I've seen on the internet, to compliment further the phenomenon of leadership by example. In the video, a soldier, fighting in the recent conflict in Eastern Ukraine, is being interviewed by a reporter. While he's describing the current situation on the front lines, a terrifying sound of incoming rocket artillery interrupts the conversation. As most of the soldiers can be seen in the background, scurrying and rushing towards the nearby building for cover, this guy just stands there, puffing away on his cigarette, paying basically no mind to the impending rain of death. And then the most interesting thing happens; the last soldier to head towards cover can be seen turning around, and upon seeing the fearlessness of his comrade, he comes around and changes his mind – staying outside. For me, this was a shining example of how courage, much like fear, spreads from one person to the next like wildfire.

Given that these soldiers were most likely regulars or volunteers, and by no means spec-ops, imagine the courage instilled into the likes of Navy SEALs, who dedicate their lives to perfecting the arts of courage and battle. Evidence of this is the many commendations won by this relatively young unit. As a matter of fact, quite a few SEALs have been awarded the Medal of

Honor in the past few decades, the highest existing decoration in the US military. Keep in mind that this is despite the generally covert and secretive nature of their operations. We will touch upon some of these stories of heroism as we go along.

If most people have a very hard time managing their emotions, consider just how tough Navy SEALs are in this regard considering the challenging conditions under which they need to master and control their emotions.

Navy SEALs are some of the world's bravest men. And you know what their secret is? Habituation. If you can learn how to use the principle of habituation, you can master your fears and live life to the fullest!

HABITUATION

One of the reasons why successful SEALs candidates are relatively fearless compared to the rest of the human race is due to their training, which employs a psychological technique called habituation. This refers to the practice of exposing a person to things that he's normally scared of. As that person is repeatedly exposed to such fear, he starts to get used to it and the fear starts to lose power over him. Eventually, he becomes immune to the things he fears and overcomes them. This is essentially mind over matter.

It's like being down 2 points with a second to go and making a 3-point shot with a defender's arms and hands in front of your face. It's approaching that woman you've been admiring for so long from a distance to introduce yourself and ask her out.

Because the primary weapons systems for any modern army are its people's minds, successfully becoming a Navy Seal is not all about how physically fit you are. Yes, it's crucial that you are extremely physically fit but being so is just a prerequisite for becoming a Navy Seal. As mentioned earlier, many candidates either quit or fall out of the program due to mental weaknesses, which includes controlling or managing one's fears.

It is widely believed that human adaptability knows no bounds. This virtue of our species has roots within our evolutionary path, but it is best exemplified by our dissemination throughout the world, in all climates and conditions where we thrive. But more importantly for our context here, this applies on the individual level as well. Namely, our ability to train our minds to function under virtually any degree of strain and hardship has gotten us to where we are. We are no longer guided by mere instinct but have the cognitive ability to analyze situations and pinpoint those that make us fearful and reluctant. We have the mental tools to surmount practically any hurdle we may encounter.

FEAR AND THE BRAIN

Whenever we encounter threats and danger, our brain has an automated system that's activated before we're able to consciously act on such threats and danger, which serves as our powerful self-defense mechanism. And this system is nestled in our amygdala.

The amygdala is that part of our brain that was developed just before the thinking or conscious part called neocortex. The amygdala is part of our brain's limbic system, the purpose of which is to manage our emotional responses or reactions like aggression and fear. Just like with social hierarchies, seniority is also a factor in terms of who gets first dibs at stuff when it comes to our responses to dangerous and threatening situations. The amygdala, together with the limbic system, is older than the neocortex (evolutionary speaking, that is) and as such; the limbic system and the amygdala often have first dibs in terms of determining our emotional responses to threats and danger. In other words, our subconscious reactions often precede conscious ones.

Consider when you first approached the girl you've had a crush on for the longest time. Wasn't it that despite your best efforts to control your nervousness (breathing slowly and deeply and relaxing your muscles), your heart was still throbbing like powered sub-woofers in a club and your throat started to dry up? That's what the limbic and amygdala's seniority looks like.

A more practical example is this. Have you ever watched one of those shows that feature people pranking others with firecrackers or by surprising them when they least expected it? How did the "victims" react? They either shrieked or screamed for a second or two before being able to control their actions. That's the amygdala at work. No matter how hard they tried to control their reactions, being surprised showed just how much faster the amygdala is in terms of controlling a person's reactions.

At this point, can you see that when it comes to situations where you feel threatened or are in danger, the two parts of your brain that struggle for control are the *neocortex*, a.k.a., the frontal lobes, which is the area responsible for your rational and conscious decisions and actions and the *amygdala*, which is an area that's deep inside the brain and is at least twice as fast in terms of reacting to protect yourself?

This is the age-old battle that keeps raging within us. It is the conflict between the evolved and the primal, between the rational and irrational, animalistic and human. As we grow to understand the concept and the inner workings of fear better and better, it will become simpler to learn how to defeat it more easily. Besides, great headway has already been made towards mastering our impulsive reactions. This is evident by the success of military forces such as the Navy SEALs, yes, but science is also hard at work to develop this area even further.

Studies conducted by the University of California and Harvard have made headway in terms of unmasking the mysterious creatures called remembered and primal fears. Experts have long thought that learned or acquired "fears" are to the amygdala, a crucial part of the brain in terms of memories, like bubble gum is to hair – stuck! Two experts from the University of Puerto Rico's medical school, Kevin Corcoran and Gregory Quirk, discovered that forming new memories in the pre-frontal cortex, another crucial area of the brain for memories, could overlay or supersede bad memories stored in the amygdala, such as fear. The Navy SEALs use this to impart the ability to master fear to their candidates by having them repeat actions that involve things most people fear over and over and over, believing that this enables candidates to "unlearn" bad memories and fears. As is, all things are experientially neutral. It is how they're interpreted by the person experiencing it that makes it good or bad.

Neuroscientists and expert psychologists currently agree that consistently confronting one's fears, triggers, memories or stimuli, is the key to successfully controlling or managing fears. Exposure therapy can cure up to 90% of people who suffer from specific phobias or extreme fears, according to Boston University's Center for Anxiety and Related Disorders director David Barlow. With this in mind, the key to courage, at least as far as the Navy SEALs are concerned, is to simply face fears and challenging situations head on day in and day out, week in and week out until the fears lose their power.

Essentially, what they attempt to do is to bend the body's software in such a manner that they manage to control its hardware. As it should be obvious by now, the physical tests that SEALs go through is nowhere near as painful as the mental torture they dish out; one must toughen up or one will fail to pass their BUDs. The SEALs firmly believe that man's strongest weapon is not the armor or the gun he has, but the mind that he has trained to react in split seconds. If you are mentally tough, then anything within your vicinity can be turned into a weapon or a tool to protect you; being smart, being present and being powerful in spite of any pain you are in – this is the kind of mental toughness the SEALs aim to train their men into.

To expand further on the previous ideas of the brain and 'unlearning' your memories – it is basically adaptation and evolution at work. Earlier on, the general belief among psychologists was that once an animal – or person, in this case – learned that it should be afraid of something that memory, stored in the amygdala will never vanish. This belief was proved to be wrong, as we saw – Quirk and Corcoran figured out that we could supersede our bad memories with better and good ones. You just need to replace the memories in your amygdala.

So how do you do this? By exposing yourself again and again to the thing that scares you constantly. You must repeat the action over and over, understanding firmly that you are conquering your fears, that you are 'unlearning' a learned behavior. And you need to dig deeper into yourself to fight your fear – try to understand why you are afraid of this particular situation. After all, most fears stem from a lack of understanding; that comprehension is the first step to facing it.

The truth, as I mentioned, is that no experience is actually good or bad – it just is. It is your perception of the experience that makes it a good or a bad memory. This is why different people have different reactions to the same things; a person is fond of the outdoors and exercise may enjoy falling down a few times when he's learning how to ski for the first time, but someone who hates that kind of experience will probably file the memory away under 'bad times' in his brain. This means that your fear is exclusive only to you and you are the only person who can conquer it.

The kind of exposure therapy the SEALs offer helps them overcome them fears to an enormous extent. When you are placed constantly in something that terrifies you, you slowly begin to overcome it, either because you understand it or you adapt to it. You may not like it and it may even still scare to an extent, but it will not paralyze you with fear as it has for so long.

Human beings have an enormous ability to adapt to a situation – we have a resilience inherent within us as mammals that has allowed us to evolve into a powerful, sentient race over the eons we have been alive on earth. The problem is that this inherent trait is buried somewhere deep inside and has become lost in the cluttered chaos of everyday life. In the SEALs, being kept away from that pitter-patter of civilization, you learn to rediscover that inherent strength within you, being forced to face your fears as you are.

So when you put yourself into the situation that scares you again and again, day in and day out, you will slowly adapt to the circumstances. You will begin to emotionally detach yourself from that which scares you – you understand it and then your response to it becomes more positive than negative. The more you expose yourself to it, the easier it becomes, until you become a part of the environment itself. And when you are part of the very situation that scares you, you become immune to your fear.

This is one of the things that separates us from animals and testifies to the fact that we have far surpassed any known species in the course of our evolution. As you have just learned, the unconscious brain is the perpetrator in that it learns to get triggered by a given situation, object, environment, etc. When an animal attains this trigger, it will remain forever ingrained in its brain. It is obvious why we, as humans, are no longer enslaved by these mechanisms. In spite of our primal instincts still persisting, our cognitive functions have evolved through all bounds and have gifted us with the ability to analyze and understand natural processes, and most importantly, solve problems.

That is exactly what our fear reaction mechanisms are – a problem. Luckily it is a problem that we keep getting better at solving, in turn making us an even sturdier and more adaptable species than we already are. Our ability to get tougher mentally, instead of just physically, is the ultimate weapon at our disposal.

The difference between a man who completes the BUD training and the man who doesn't is this mental toughness. Given that they have overcome their fears, these men learn how to bend their situation to their will; you take your fear and turn it into a weapon that you can make use of to protect yourself. The fear becomes a tool to solve problems, instead of crippling and paralyzing you. They are ready to do whatever they have to survive and protect, and they learn to use their fear to make those split second decisions that could mean a person's life.

OVERCOMING FEAR, THE NAVY SEALS WAY

Because life-threatening situations are part of Navy SEALs regular diets, they're the very first people who need to keep their emotions, particularly fears, under control. As such, who else to best learn fear control from than the Navy SEALs? When it comes to doing so, they utilize a technique known as The Big Four, which as the name suggests has four parts: goals, visualization, positive self-talk, and arousal control.

One of the many outstanding examples of incredible valor displayed by a Navy SEAL surely is the story of Michael A. Monsoor. Namely, this courageous individual has exemplified the ability to conquer the ultimate of fears – the fear of death. And not only did he sacrifice his life for his country, but for his comrades. In September of 2006, Monsoor and his teammates, along with their Iraqi allies, found themselves engaged in a firefight against Ramadi insurgents from their rooftop sniper position. In the course of the ensuing battle, an enemy frag grenade found its way onto the roof, ending up right in front of him. Without any hesitation, Monsoor threw himself on top of the grenade, fully absorbing the impact of the explosion, saving his comrades from certain death. This gallant act earned him a posthumous Medal of Honor and an eternal place among legends. Needless to say, this kind of split-second action, and complete disregard for one's own safety goes to show that this is not about glory or recognition, as nobody thinks about these things in such a dire situation. It is almost a reflex action towards sacrifice and selflessness. Whether this virtue is learned or innate, it lies beyond my comprehension and limited wisdom.

- GOALS
- VISUALIZATION
- POSITIVE SELF-TALK
- AROUSAL CONTROL

Imagine the frame of mind and the sort of character of a man who makes this decision in a split second, selflessly sacrificing his own life without any second thoughts, only to protect his teammates. This degree of valor surpasses any notions of patriotism, and instead represents the purity of courageous spirit, and is the very epitome of sacrifice and dedication to the man next to you in combat.

In the interest of our Earthly subject of conquering fear in everyday life, which pales in comparison to the aforementioned heroism, we'll take a more detailed look into each of the four components within the SEAL technique called The Big Four. Although you probably won't be smothering grenades and earning medals any time soon, this is no reason not to learn from the best and get an edge on life.

Goals

Goal setting is as common to successful people as breathing is to living. But the difference between ordinary successful people and Navy SEALs is that the SEALs' goals aren't general or opaque, they're very detailed and specific. Just how specific? Consider that their goals are broken down into micro, short-term, mid-term and long-terms goals.

An example of just how specific Navy SEALs can be in terms of setting goals, consider the way they treat their BUDS training program. Instead of looking at it as one, 6-month long program, successful candidates broke it down into weekly, daily, hourly and even per-minute goals! An example of this is their 90-minute grinder sessions, which are performed at 6 in the morning prior to having breakfast. They focus on successfully finishing that 90-minute session before they even think of anything else. They even break it down further into sets, which they completely focus on. The process of breaking down their goals to as small as extremely possible units that are very specific and simple, allows their mind focus undistracted on one goal at a time. It's this practice of setting short-term and micro-level goals and combining these with longer-term, more general goals that sets Navy SEALs apart from the rest of the human race in terms of controlling and managing fears for personal success.

So how can you apply it to your personal life? Consider making a list of things you need to do on a daily basis. Instead of looking at your schedule on a daily basis, look at it from a more micro level or per task. Like the successful Navy SEALs candidates, focus your energy and attention on just one task at a time before moving on to the next. Refuse to move on to your next item unless you're done with the current one as much as possible. Doing so trains your mind to be relentless in pursuing a goal, just like how Navy SEALs are when on missions.

Many of us will focus too hard on our long-term goal and end up stumbling over smaller and more imminent tasks along the way. Think of it as walking towards a certain goal a few miles away. On what do you focus as you walk? Of course, you will always look at what's right in front of you; otherwise, you'd trip on something in your path. Absolutely, this simple philosophy can be successfully applied in life to great effect. By taking things one small task or goal at a time, you may not even notice how far you went along your way, and just how much you've accomplished in a small period of time.

Visualization

World-class performers and athletes have long used visualization, also known as mental practice, to get better and better at their crafts by augmenting actual physical rehearsals. In fact, many performance psychologists believe that visualization is as important as physical practice in terms of achieving peak performance. During the BUDS training program, candidates who excel tend to practice visualization.

Case in point: the Second Phase of BUDS training. One of the training exercises that candidates are required to do is performing various corrective actions and emergency procedures for handling problematic underwater situations with scuba equipment while underwater. Further, their instructors disconnect their equipment while doing so in order to simulate the worst-case scenario of being left deep beneath the water without equipment. If the candidate seems to be too tense or anxious during the exercise, the instructor fails that candidate. This is one of the most challenging graded exercises in BUDS training.

The candidates who excelled and passed the exercise on the first go prepared for it by watching mental movies of themselves performing the necessary corrective actions while being attacked underwater. And because they already "saw" the performance and the attacks in their minds beforehand, their minds were ready by the time the actual scenarios unfolded, which gave them full control over their mental and physical faculties on their way to excellently passing the exercise on the first try.

You can do the same with just about any challenging task or situation that gives you the heebie-jeebies or makes you afraid or anxious. Is it conducting a sales pitch to your first big-ticket prospect? Imagine yourself confidently, persuasively and eloquently pitching your product or service to your prospective big-ticket clients and anticipate every possible, and even scary, questions that they may throw at you. By doing so, you significantly reduce the possibility of being blind-sided by difficult questions or challenging remarks and increases your chances of successfully pitching to your potentially first big-ticket account.

As a matter of fact, it may be most important to visualize all the ways in which the situation can go wrong and get out of hand. You should even get creative when imagining all of the possible glitches and disasters, which may strike. With each calamity you dream up, work hard on developing a corresponding solution and course of action through which you will get past the problem. This would work a lot like getting ready for a test with a list of possible questions, making sure you know the answer to each and every one!

Positive Self-Talk

Believe it or not, you actually talk to yourself several times daily. It's just that you're unaware when you do it. But that shouldn't actually worry you. What should is the fact that not all of the things you tell yourself are positive or build you up. Some of them are negative or tear you down such as:

"You're not good enough to win that account!"

"You're not man enough for that chick you're in love with!"

"You're not smart enough to get into that university!"

Interestingly, successful Navy SEALs candidates that passed BUDS training learned to block out all forms of negative self-talk and only spoke positive affirmations to themselves for motivation and empowerment. One of the ways they talk positively to themselves is by reminding themselves that of countless others who have gone before them were able to complete the training program, so can they. They remind themselves that given their superior physical conditioning, there should be no reason why they can't pass the BUDS physical screening tests. Lastly, they're their own drill sergeants when they yell to themselves never to quit no matter what.

So how does this translate to your personal life? You may not go through the same hellish situations that Navy SEALs go through but keep in mind that the word "hellish" is relative. Your situations may not be, as life threatening as those of the Navy SEALs but it doesn't mean you don't need positive self-talk. You do.

It's as simple as refraining from telling yourself or others things that put you down or downplays your skills and abilities. There's a huge difference between positive self-talk and arrogance. You can be both humble and talk positively to yourself. Arrogance is telling yourself "No one can beat me in this game because the competition sucks." while positive self-talk says to yourself that "I can win over any opponent because I worked hard at mastering the game and I take my opponents' skill levels seriously."

Positive self-talk isn't just about when you're facing or about to face challenging situations. You perform it on yourself as often as possible. The more frequently you talk positively to yourself, the faster you can be more confident and control your fears and anxieties.

A lot of people actually do this without even thinking about it. The unconscious, positive self-talk is usually very basic, brief and doesn't do much in the way of confidence. The trick is to make a conscious effort to analyze your qualities, virtues, and advantages, to be able to find an objective basis for your conviction that you can succeed – and, believe me, you can find this basis. If you are trying to reach a particular goal, that means you already possess the essential qualities to achieve it. It's all about pinpointing those qualities and reminding yourself that you do, in fact, have what it takes, until your resolve hardens further.

— NEVER QUIT NO MATTER WHAT

Arousal Control

Part of mental resiliency is the ability to control arousal or responses to outside stimuli (arousal) such as danger and excitement. This is because in order to power through pain, suffering and fear, one must be able to keep himself from being controlled by his body and must be able to control his response to such stimuli. Part of this response is the emotion of fear. Navy SEALs learn to control their psychological as well as their physiological responses to external stimuli during their trainings.

Here's how it works. Our bodies release certain chemicals like endorphins and cortisol whenever it senses dangers and threats or if overwhelmed. The release of such chemicals is what causes our bodily functions to malfunction, our hearts to pound like subwoofers in a club, our minds to race as if they're Formula One cars and our palms to sweat as if they were in a sauna. While they're natural stress and danger responses, the ability to control these stimuli arousals for Navy SEALs to maintain poise even in the most stressful, dangerous and even exciting mission situations and environments.

Remember, it's not about the absence of fear, fear is okay, and it is completely natural. There is no man alive who simply isn't afraid of anything in life, but this becomes irrelevant once you learn to conduct yourself despite this fear and function as if you are in any other, normal situation. That's what courage is, keeping your fears at bay or even working for you, operating no matter how intense they become.

One technique that Navy SEALs use to control their arousals, which you can use as well to control your fears, is the 4X4. It's a breathing technique where you deeply inhale for 4 seconds and exhale steadily over the next 4 seconds, repeating for at least 1 minute for maximum calming effect.

Breathing has long been established as an effective means of suppressing bouts of anxiety or fighting milder panic attacks in psychiatric practice. Hiking up your oxygen intake and getting a strong grip on your lungs is crucial in these situations due to the simple fact that a deliberate surge of oxygen to your brain will help maintain cognitive function as much as possible. At moments when we feel anxious or afraid we may not even notice that we have actually stopped breathing, this can not only impede on your brain's activity but can manifest some physical problems as well, such

CONTROL THE PSYCHOLOGICAL AND PHYSIOLOGICAL
4X4 BREATHING TECHNIQUE - 1 MINUTE

as trembling or even fainting. Employing the 4x4 breathing effort can help in those dire situations, let alone in simpler ones where there isn't that much of a threat to begin with.

So the next time you feel anxiety kicking in as you approach that beautiful woman you've always been meaning to ask out or as you step up onstage to give your first public speech, take a minute or two to do the 4X4 so you can control your fear and succeed in your endeavor.

CHAPTER 6: RESILIENCE

If you carefully observe the Navy SEALs, you'll notice that one of their best tactics for achieving the seemingly impossible things is sheer determination or resilience to keep on going on with their missions despite being saddled with just about any conceivable snag, accident or unforeseen situational changes. They've learned that failure to quickly get back on their feet after experiencing massive and crippling failures has very dire consequences. Training through failures with the expectations of winning develops resiliency.

Before we delve into the ways of applying this virtue to our daily lives and pursuit of success, let us reflect on another true story of bravery and resilience, yet again shown by a Medal of Honor recipient from the ranks of Navy SEALs.

Remember the 2005 "Operation Red Wings," which we mentioned in chapter 4? Well, the man of the hour – or rather, this chapter – is Lt. Michael P. Murphy, who died along with two other teammates from his squad where Marcus Luttrell was the sole survivor. As his four-man team came under a deadly ambush in the Kunar Province of Afghanistan, orchestrated by a much larger militia force, Murphy and his men became engaged in a deadly clash through the harsh, mountainous terrain. While making their way down the slopes of the mountain and toward a local village, the team stopped in cover to attempt to call in reinforcements.

After taking a suitable defense position and cover, casualties began to mount on both sides and as it was quickly discovered, the adverse terrain made communication next to impossible. As the team's communications officer fell, and others became wounded, Murphy kept trying to reach out to their HQ, but to no avail. Stricken by the peril of his men, and acutely aware of the danger, Lt. Murphy stormed into open terrain and directly into the incoming enemy fire in order to establish contact with command. While bullets were cracking all around him, he used his sat-phone and successfully reached the HQ, relaying the call for help. Upon getting shot through the chest area, the device fell out of his hands, but he picked it back up and confirmed the transmission, and only after the exchange did he make his way back to his team in cover! Unfortunately, the next time he was hit he fell dead.

TRAINING THROUGH FAILURES WITH THE EXPECTATIONS OF WINNING DEVELOPS RESILIENCY

Michael P. Murphy was 29 years old at the time of his heroic death, and the first Navy serviceman since the Vietnam War to receive the highest decoration in the military.

The devotion to duty and camaraderie which has been shown here serves to demonstrate further what the Navy SEAL ethos is all about. Furthermore, this particular act and others like it exemplify that which a resilient and highly motivated individual can do. Again, comparing any hardships of daily life to the horrors of war is out of the question, but such extreme cases show you just how far the resilience of character can take a man. This is why this virtue is held in high regard among the SEALs.

Simply put, resiliency is crucial for personal success, especially if you're chasing lofty goals. The following steps can help you develop Navy SEALs-like resiliency for powering through very difficult and challenging situations and coming out successfully on top.

IDENTIFICATION

You can't control or manage your emotional reactions and develop resiliency if you're not aware of them in the first place. Therefore, identifying and witnessing your negative reactions as they arise is the crucial first step. Whenever you feel afraid, anxious or distressed, notice how you emotionally react. Does your heart palpitate? Does your breathing become shallow? Do you snap out easily towards others? It is important to be self-critical and objective during this process. You may find quite a few weaknesses in your character. This is something that can and should be fixed, but you must acknowledge these shortcomings in order to address them adequately. A little self-honesty goes a long way towards improving your performance in life.

GET TO THE ROOT

After you've identified or witnessed your particular emotional reactions to challenging situations, get to the bottom of it. In other words, find out why you're feeling and responding that way, the roots. Often times, identifying the emotional root is enough to help a person overcome their emotional reactions and become resilient in the face of overwhelming challenges and odds. This is where the art of introspection comes in. Some people's entire lives are spent in introspection, which can sometimes be tormenting for an individual, but it is important to be able to do this nonetheless. Looking deep inside yourself without any lens will show you many aspects of your personality upon which you can improve.

The art of introspection, as I just referred to it, works only if you are honest with yourself, though. Just as is the case with anything else in life, it is important to remain objective and realistic, never sugar coating things for personal comfort. If you feel that you have a certain problem with yourself, you most likely do have it. But, if you approach it with honesty and constructive criticism towards yourself, you will certainly be able to fix it. One thing you can be completely sure of when it comes to your inner self is that you are in complete control, but it may sometimes be hard to get in touch with this truth and make it begin working to your advantage.

The goal of identifying the root is to examine it and experience it fully and not to deny or avoid it. Running away from root emotions or situations that challenge you won't develop resiliency in you but will make you even less resilient. If resiliency is about strength to persist in the midst of challenges, then it follows that you'll need to practice the principle of habituation to get develop resilient strength and weaken the power of challenging situations over you. This means wrestling your problems head-on instead of sweeping them under the rug. Any successful person in history will vouch for this course, especially men capable of graduating Navy SEAL training.

COUNTERSTRIKE

Only by experiencing such emotions fully can you be in the position to attack the crippling emotion or situation and develop greater resiliency. So what does it mean to counterstrike?

If you feel scared about a situation, say attending social functions where you don't know anybody, you can counterstrike by attending such functions more frequently in order to get used to such situations through the habituation technique previously discussed. If you often times feel angry and stressed when buying from a particular grocery store and a particular cashier, buy from that store and cashier as often as possible in order for you to get used to it and handle your emotional responses well.

It's about pushing yourself beyond your initial limits. This is where mental and physical exercises overlap. Think of it like running; the harder you try and the more you run, the greater the distances you can overcome as time goes by. In turn, your shape keeps improving and you become stronger each time.

POSITIVE SELF-TALK

Lastly, do as the Navy SEALs do and engage yourself often with positive self-talk. Remember how we talked about it in Chapter 5 on courage? You can do the same to be encouraged during very discouraging times. Sometimes, your inner attitude toward yourself can be more deciding than what others might say about you, whether their comments are encouraging or the opposite. Many prosperous people throughout history really owe their success to themselves and themselves only. These individuals have often had to face harsh criticism and discouragement from others, but their inner voice was stronger and louder than anything others could spout – and thus they prevailed.

CHAPTER 7: MENTAL FITNESS

The brain, despite its lack of physiological firmness compared to other physical muscles, is probably the strongest one there is. Why? Think of it this way, you can't move your physical muscles if this muscle is not working. Further, consider the stories of many people who were able to do the seemingly impossible acts of heroism they performed if they weren't mentally tough. Some Navy SEALs were seriously wounded but were still able save themselves and their buddies too! Despite the pain, their brains were able to override the sensations and allowed them to function at an even higher physical level and perform what seemed to be downright impossible. Mental preparation is key for such feats and allows you to significantly exceed your own personal "limits". At least your perceived ones.

Many of the limits we impose on ourselves are artificial. They are either falsely brought on by our insecurities and irrational fears or by the remarks of others, sometimes those closest and most influential to us. Through sufficient mental exercise and specific processes of thought, we can surmount these illusive limits as well as those that may actually be there.

The world is full of shining examples where highly disadvantaged and horribly afflicted people have overcome their very real limitations through sheer mental strength and determination. Sports, for instance, are an area where many strong-willed people have found their fortune.

Since the brain is a muscle, it can also be trained to become stronger with brain-specific exercises that, unlike physical muscles, don't need barbells, dumbbells or resistance bands. You can do mental exercises anytime and anywhere. Here are ways how you can exercise your mind for optimal performance and toughness ala-Navy SEALs.

Essentially, to exercise your brain, all you need is a brain. I'm going to go out on a limb here and assume that you have this covered. All kidding aside, these techniques will show you just how easy and exactly how beneficial these exercises are.

BATTLE-PROOFING

This refers to the military practice of conditioning the mind in advance for encountering possible emergencies or hostile situations, which helps produce the necessary mental strength for crises management. This is also called emergency conditioning.

Navy SEALs in training practice this by, among other ways, lying on their cots and imagining that an intense firefight is currently ongoing. Part of this imagining process includes the sounds, scents, the sense of physical exhaustion and heavy breathing.

Why is this helpful? It's because when our brains vividly and deeply imagine things in detail, they eventually form part of our experiences, regardless if they actually happened or just in our minds. The brain can't tell the difference and battle proofing your brain can program your brain into believing that you really experienced that which you've imagined! Over time, you can develop the ability to tap into those stored experiences, which you can play like mini movies of what you'd like to experience. So when similar situations arise, you feel familiar with it already.

The visualization techniques we mentioned in chapter 5 are the civilian version, if you will, of this military practice. If you focus hard enough to envision these experiences before they happen, whatever they may be, it will be the next best thing to a simulation. Our brains are that powerful, and visualizing upcoming events perceived as stressful is a great way of mental preparation to maximize readiness and help you pull through.

What happens is very simple – your brain comes up with the images in great detail. The more detailed it is, the better entrenched in your mind it becomes, so much so that it becomes part of your 'experience files' and not just an imaginary situation. This kind of visualization will actually fool your brain into thinking that you have actually undergone this event in life. It is sort of like a computer; you just need to access this file and then click on 'start' – the memory is something you can relive enough times to get yourself familiar with the fear and overcome it. This way, when something similar happens in real life, you are battle-proofed enough that you don't freeze up when required. You take quick and prompt action that could potentially save other people's lives.

TRIGGERS

Part of the necessary things for preparing yourself mentally for challenges is creating your "trigger", which can help you ignite into flame those qualities necessary not just for "survival" but for personal success. You'll need to dig down deep into your soul, determine that one most important thing in your life and create a mental portrait of it. This mental portrait will act as your trigger for fanning the flame of resiliency during moments when you'd rather just roll over and die or give up. It can also trigger in you the creativity and patience needed for overcoming certain situations.

For a father who works abroad and away from his wife and kids, his trigger maybe a picture of the family he's left behind. Whenever extreme loneliness sets in, he simply looks at his family picture to remind him why he must persist there, to provide well for their needs back home.

For Navy SEALs, these triggers can also be their families. It can also be the United States flag, knowing that if they fail, terrorists may win and destroy the American way of life for everyone, including their families. Moreover, the responsibility towards their comrades and brothers in arms, the fact that the actions of each team member directly affect not only the outcome of the mission but the wellbeing and safety of their teammates.

So how can you apply it to your own personal life? Think about that which is most important to you? Is it God, your spouse, kids, parents, friends or some noble cause? Create a mental image of that one most important thing for you that you can visualize whenever you feel the need for a resiliency shot in the arm, among other things, in situations that make you want to throw in the towel.

These so-called triggers are an incredibly useful crutch, which you can fall back on in times of crisis and overwhelming tribulation. That which matters most to you is a lasting source of motivation and strength, and knowing when to use this can push you to achieve great things.

As you can guess, each person will have a different trigger – it has to be something that will motivate you as a person. Given your circumstances, your personality and all the things that matter to you as an individual, you need to pick a trigger that will motivate you. Spend some time alone in the wilderness to try and figure out what is most important to you. Soul searching is essential if you want to become physically and mentally tougher.

The general stereotype is that soldiers are strong, macho men who tend to brood and fight and not emote openly – this could not be more wrong. The emotional ramifications of war and fighting are enormous; soldiers, in act, tend to be more in touch with their feelings and in tune with their emotions than a normal person. The difference, though, is that they use their heightened energies to serve their country; their triggers are directed towards battle and protection. An individual can achieve full control over their emotions and conduct only through deep understanding and self-awareness, and subsequently training. Suppressing those feelings won't lead to stability and toughness, but only to an illusion of strength. And such illusions will fall apart as soon as the going gets tough, leading to panic, retreat and ultimate failure. Remember, lies are never a solid foundation to build anything on, especially when it comes to building and strengthening your character.

Some SEALs confess to their triggers being their families; a lot of men summon up images of their children or significant others to keep them on their feet and trying to get back to them. During their BUDS training, they probably imagine walking across the stage and receiving their graduation. But more often than not, SEALs tend to have their triggers be of their fellow comrades; many admit to fighting harder just to make sure that their men would come back home safe and sound. After all, if there is one thing war and military teach you, it's how to be part of a team!

So to summarize, your trigger is your own – there is no right or wrong trigger, there is no set guideline to come up with one. Dig deep into your soul; you may think the idea of having a trigger like receiving a certificate is petty, but for someone else, it could mean the whole world! Anything goes – it must just be your own and it must mean enough to you that it gets you back on your feet when you are about to drop from exhaustion.

Just keep in mind to make your visualizations extremely vivid – burn it into your mind and keep reminding yourself that you are willing to go through any kind of difficulty for this. It is your ultimate motivation. Also keep in mind that if you want it to be effective, you should save this trigger for the worst situations – for simple, everyday activities where you need to push yourself, find simpler motivations. The trigger is meant to be used only for those circumstances that you find extremely difficult to handle.

TAKING YOUR MIND OUT

Consider some of the most stressful or challenging situations that you face in ordinary everyday life. Things like missing the green light because of a very slow elderly driver in the car that's in front of you, falling in line behind a person with three carts' worth of grocery items at the checkout counter, or a very grouchy server in your favorite restaurant. These are situations where you can practice taking your mind off stressful, challenging, and time wasting situations.

This is especially important when dealing with unnecessary anger. Vexation and repressed anger build up inside every day, but only if you let them in. Sure, in some critical situations anger will be helpful; after all, it is a natural response and part of our defense mechanisms. But, our lives in today's world are such that there is rarely any real, physical danger to us, so this anger becomes completely redundant, which is no good because anger and rage are some of the heaviest baggage in life.

Being angry, irritable, and easily set-off is no way to go through life. These feelings will become very detrimental as time goes by and will make it increasingly difficult for you to get a grip on your emotions and stabilize your character. Not only is such a state of mind pointless, but the feelings associated with it are some of the most consuming and demanding we can experience. It just doesn't pay off to be angry all the time. So, starting with brief, regular encounters and situations which cause you stress or annoy you, you must begin to build your resistance and control amid the basic things, and move up from there.

Why do you need to do this? It's because some situations are unnecessary mind-fillers, i.e., they occupy space and utilize resources that can otherwise be used for more productive and important purposes. For example, have you ever experienced being cut off and screamed at by another driver while driving to work in the morning and being all worked up to the point that you couldn't concentrate well at work? The more you practice taking your mind out of situations that unnecessarily stress you out, the more you'll be able to control your personal circumstances well and become more successful at what it is you do.

WAIT

As the saying goes, good things come to those who wait. Have you ever considered the underlying meaning of this proverb? No, it doesn't mean you should procrastinate. In the narrower sense, it simply means that haste often does make waste and that you should keep a cool head and consider your options carefully, analytically. Being well informed and having a solid understanding of the circumstances and prospects you are faced with is a crucial component of successful decision-making. It's important to understand that your first idea is rarely the best your mind can come up with.

How many times have you experienced situations where you ended up responding exactly according to the first impulse or thought that popped in your head? While it's true that most people operate in this manner and that it's not necessarily a wrong way of responding, it's not the best way. Being decisive is one of the basic qualities that lead to success in life. Decisiveness doesn't mean you are merely quick to make decisions. More than that, it is the ability to make good judgments and always choose the right path in life.

There will be times that you'll need to wait for other good ideas to pop in your head before responding to certain situations. When you let this process run its course, some very good and wonderful things may result from it. The reason for this is by waiting as long as reasonably possible before responding to situations, you increase the potential options available to you by allowing more time for more ideas to develop. If you always act on the thoughts or impulses that pop in your head, there's a very good chance that those ideas or thoughts may not be the best ones. In many cases, acting on impulse often results in costly mistakes.

That's why Navy SEALs don't usually act on the first thought or impulse that pops in their minds, especially in very critical situations. They have the option of pursuing subsequent ideas or simply going back to the original one. The only thing that matters is to act on the best possible course of action for a particular situation. This only happens when you have the ability to reign in your mind and keep it from running wild.

These are the most important ways in which you can build your mental toughness, but you cannot stop there! There are a few things you need to concentrate on – these are those qualities that are important before, during and after you have completed this type of vigorous training. Military man Mark Divine, who has served over two decades as a SEAL recommends that you keep the following in mind as you begin to train your brain as well as your body –

UNDERSTAND YOURSELF

Self-awareness is the key to building a strong mind; when you know yourself, you can make better decisions. When you understand your deepest motivations, comprehend your toughest insecurities; you can avoid making the same mistakes over and over again. Instead, you can try to move forward.

As you can probably guess, building self-awareness for yourself does not come easy. It takes quite a bit of soul searching and you will need to spend a lot of time in self-reflection to make sure that you are at peace with yourself. The calmer you are at the battlefront, the better for you and your comrades.

Truly understanding yourself and, better yet, accepting what you learn and coming to terms with yourself, is truly a difficult task and quite an accomplishment. Many people struggle through the entirety of their lives just to find this peace, and many of them never succeed. For the Navy SEALs, this state of mind is not only a goal but a prerequisite for success in the line of duty. Their training programs ensure that each passing candidate has achieved this, and then some. So, once again, you can learn from the best as you strive to master yourself.

Start by recording a simple journal. Jot down random thoughts, ideas and even stray things that roll into your mind at the oddest of instances. You don't need to show it to anyone, or even reread it yourself – when you write down what you are thinking, you tend to instinctively become aware of what is happening in your mind. If you are so inclined, track the patterns of your thoughts over a period of time; you will find how predictable your reactions are and how you, as a person, perceive the world.

Set aside 10 minutes in a day for yourself – sit in a corner and try to breathe deeply. Focus inwards and try to answer existential questions like who you are and why you are where you are in life. It sounds cliché, it sounds like a trope, but believe me, and it works! Reflection is the best way to build personality – build it into your routine and then see how it helps you become more self-aware!

FIGURE OUT WHAT YOUR PURPOSE IS

As Divine states in his writing, the way your mind works has an impact on your performance in anything. Your worldview and how you take in your surroundings make an impact on your reaction to it; so you need to ask yourself – why do you do what you do? Navy SEAL or otherwise, if you don't understand the purpose behind your job, you are never going to truly enjoy or even accept it! For instance, if a man did not want to be a SEAL and ended up going through the motions because his father was also a SEAL and is pushing him to do it, do you think he would make a true asset to the team? His halfhearted notions on the battlefield will probably get either him or his comrades killed.

Ask yourself the following questions –

- What is it that you were conditioned to think you are supposed to do in life?
- What do you want to do with your life?
- What do you think you are supposed to do with your life? (This question looks similar to the previous one, but there is a very fine line between the two; think deeply about it and you will be able to understand.)
- Do you feel like your life makes no difference at all?
- Do you feel like you should be doing something else, anything other than what you are doing right now?
- In a perfect world where everything was possible and you could do whatever you wanted, what is the one thing you would do without hesitation?
- And cliché – what would you do if you knew you had only one year to live?

When you ask yourself tough questions such as these, you will be able to understand if and why you are so unhappy in your current situation. Remember, you cannot go through life half-heartedly – you can't keep going through the motions. SEALs and other military men, perhaps, live more than any of the others – as those constantly in danger of losing their lives, they know how precious life is and they generally tend to refuse to waste it by doing things they do not like. As civilians, this is one of the biggest lessons we can learn from them; be self-aware, learn to make yourself as happy as you try to make your friends and family.

CHOOSE YOUR PATH

Divine advises that each of us choose what we want to do on our own; it is definitely good advice, something that makes sense! Once you have answered all the aforementioned questions, you will have a clearer picture of who you are and where you want to be in life. Then, you can decide on a path that you can follow.

Going through life is much easier and more worthwhile if you have a clear goal and an idea of what you want to make of your life. SEALs don't have this problem, their purpose and goals are as clear as can be at all times.

Discipline, courage, determination and a capacity to keep at it – developing all these things is what SEAL life teaches us, but to for that, you first need to identify where you are headed. Learn yourself onside out and then see where life takes you.

BECOME PART OF A WHOLE

As I've said before, one of the most important lessons we learn from the Navy SEALs is the spirit of teamwork and brotherhood that exists between them. When some one is willing to die for you on a battlefield, you obviously learn to trust them with everything you have. Obviously, such bonds are harder to forge in civilian life, but they can be done, providing you take the time to try it out.

Once you have figured out your path in life, you must stay on it. This is easier said than done; anything that is worth doing never comes easy. A lot of people give up halfway through the process because they are too tired or don't have the strength to keep going. Augment your own efforts by supporting and getting support from a team – search for people who are going through struggles similar to yours and encourage one another to complete your goals. Staying on the path you have chosen for yourself is much easier when you have some one cheering you on from the back!

Here are a few more tips to keep in mind as you are trying to build up your mental and emotional strength –

- Have faith in yourself; clichéd as it sounds, this belief in your own mind is what the basis of mental conditioning actually is. If you don't have confidence in yourself and your own abilities, you will never be able to achieve all you want in life. It is easier said than done, but it is not impossible! Navy SEALs often use bodybuilding as a technique to boost confidence among their men; they set themselves simple, easy to achieve goals in the physical training field. You too can try it out – don't expect too much from yourself at one go and take it day-by-day and step-by-step. For instance, if you're just beginning physical conditioning, make your goal something as simple as working out for 30 minutes for two weeks. Cross each day out on your calendar and then when you're done with the two week period, notice how much more confident you feel in yourself! Now up your routine to a 45 minute set or do two 30 minute sets a day – keep it small, keep it simple and work daily towards it and your confidence levels will go up.
- Focus on the present. We generally tend to live either in the past or in the future, missing out on what today has to offer us completely. In the battlefield, thinking about what a SEAL could have done differently to save someone's life – which kind of regret and inaction could get another person killed or hurt. There is no room for distraction, from the past or the future; the soldiers have to focus on getting to safety in this exact instant or they run the risk of being hurt. Transpose this lesson into your life; focus only on what you need to do today and try to enjoy that to the maximum. The past is over and you cannot retrieve or fix it – the future is not here yet, so why waste precious time worrying about it? Easy it sounds, easy it is not to do – just keep your attention on the solid things you're doing right now. Go to the gym, work out and feel your body and your muscles – the pain will centre you and keep you fresh and feeling alive in the moment.
- Keep positive company around you. As we mentioned, SEALs are a team – they push each other and support one another to get things done. If one cannot trust his team, one goes into the battle blind and ends up, at the very least, hurt or critically injured. The same applies to civilian life; the people in your life can make or break you. Surround yourself with positive energy and people who are like-minded and push you to do better, to become a better person. Don't get stuck in a rut with someone negative; you will find that your goals seem unattainable, too far and too painful to fight for.
- Learn to control your breathing. SEALs are taught this as an essential measure of battling panic and chaos on the field; the mind is like a little puppy that needs constant reassurance. When take in shallow breaths and

rapidly increase your breathing, your brain automatically ends up in chaos, leaving your gut churning with anxiety and worry. Biologically speaking, the reason for this is simple – shallow breathing equals lesser oxygen intake, which means your brain, is literally starving for air. Learn to breathe in deeply – have your lungs and diaphragm expand laterally so that you take in as much oxygen as possible. This will help you calm down and think better so that you can make those tough, split second decisions that could mean the difference between life and death.

Navy SEALs are the toughest men out there – for good reason. They are strong, but their strength comes as much from their mind as it does their body. In fact, they use their body to build their mind further; learn to do the same so that you can also face the tough situations in your life!

CHAPTER 8: CROSS FIT TRAINING

We looked at some cardio and calisthenics that you can take up; now, we shall focus on cross fit training, which is a form of high intensity interval training. Cross fit training is a type of high intensity interval training where you subject your body to intense exercises for a period of time and then take a break, train again, break again and so on.

Cross fit is strength conditioning set of exercises that is generally prescribed to police academies, military units and Special Forces. This makes it a must to take up activity for a navy seal.

Cross fit training works on the principle of indulging in surge fitness. This means that you push your body first before taking a break and then push it again and break again. This causes the body to develop resistance and can endure a tough situation.

Each training episode will bring your body further towards a fit and sturdy state. Given that cross fit is one of the most zealous forms of training, sustained and dedicated exercise will take you far and take you there fast. Within a relatively short period of working out, you will begin to see just how adaptable human beings are.

As your resistance increases, you will ramp up the strain you put on your body every time, gradually raising the intensity of each session. The biggest advantage of this training program, besides its versatility, is the fact that it can be taken up regardless of your physical state and level of fitness. What this means is that irrespective of the individual, the aim is to push your body to its limits before taking a break. It matters not how low your limits may be at the time, a prolonged and disciplined approach to this exercise will improve anybody's durability and shape.

Here are the areas that will be targeted during a cross fit regime.

Cardiovascular strength

Cross fit training starts by checking your cardio vascular health. As you know, it is important for you to maintain a healthy heart in order to develop endurance. Cross fit will help you with the same.

Think of your heart as the main generator of your body. The lengths to which you can push yourself depend on how efficient your heart is at its crucial job. A well-functioning cardiovascular system is the absolute cornerstone of a healthy body. The better the blood supply to your muscles, the more power you are able to harness from them to get you as far as you can possibly go.

The difference between an actual generator and this central human muscle, of course, is that your heart can be exercised, constantly improving its performance.

Stamina

Your stamina deals with your lasting energy. When it comes to cross fit training, you need a good dose of stamina to last the entire workout. As you go about, your stamina will continually increase. BUD/S will require you to possess great stamina!

Stamina primarily represents the ceiling to which your performance can peak. With SEALs, stamina can mean the difference between life and death, not only of one's self, but of comrades just as well. Granted, it most likely won't come to that in the course of your own life, but if it saves lives, then it's a road to success. Not to mention, it is an unavoidable prerequisite for further exercise and physical development.

Strength

You will require immense upper and lower body strength to take up the different cross fit exercises. Working on these two areas will allow you to quickly assume demanding positions without putting in too much effort towards it.

While it isn't the only factor in becoming nimble and well coordinated, physical strength is definitely part of the equation as it translates to power. The sheer force of power does come into speed and quick reaction. More importantly, though, the stronger you are the further you can take your exercise sessions.

Flexibility

You have to be flexible in order to swiftly move from position to the other. As is the case with most high intensity training workouts, here too, you will have to quickly move from one position to the other. It will help you do the same while serving your duty.

You are highly unlikely to find yourself dodging bullets and rocket-propelled grenades in your ordinary, civilian life. Here, flexibility plays a different role than that in combat. Being flexible will aid your exercise sessions in that it reduces the risk of injury or embarrassment. Feeling nimble also does your confidence a service and will make any sports you take up much more fun and worthwhile.

Power

There is a difference between strength and power. Strength refers to your body's capacity to perform the basic exercises whereas power refers to understanding how well and efficiently you can perform them. Power basically refers to the next step.

Speed

As mentioned earlier, cross fit will make you change your positions within short bursts. Therefore, you have to be ready to move from one position to the other within a short period of time and for that, speed will play a key role. You have to have the agility to move from one position to the other within express time.

The faster you become, the more assured you will be of your ability to act quickly and precisely, and when you couple that with coordination and accuracy, you will become better aware of your own body, so to speak. What that means is control, composure, and confidence. It's about being 100% sure that you can make that jump or beat that clock.

Balance

Balance is of utmost importance for most exercise regimes. You have to balance your body at all times and also maintain your steady form. Cross fit training can help you have this and more. It will leave you feeling extremely stable and capable of remaining physically steady during any mission.

More precisely, exercise balance is important in that it ensures you don't go too far on one aspect of your fitness while neglecting another. It means balancing between agility, raw strength, speed, stamina and all other components of a healthy body. Navy SEALs understand this, having too much muscle mass while neglecting to improve your stamina, for example, will leave you slow and easily exhausted.

Coordination

It requires a certain level of co-ordination when it comes to taking up cross fit training. This can be both body co-ordination and hand-eye co-ordination. You will get good with it as and when you take up the practice. Another crucial component of becoming a fit and overall nimble individual, coordination is something that, for the most part, comes naturally through physical exercise. You can take up specific activities to dedicate more effort towards improving your coordination, though. This can be done efficiently through many forms of sport, which require accuracy and developing a keener sense of your own arms and legs. Basketball and soccer, to name a couple, can improve your coordination to great lengths, and not only that but they will help you develop a firmer control over the amount of force you exert during exercise.

Accuracy

You have to be as accurate as possible in order to successfully adopt the different cross fit positions.

Cross fit training has its own set of words that you have to acquaint yourself with when you wish to take up the practice. Here is looking at some of them. WOD- WOD stands for work out of the day. Cross-fit makes you pick a routine and perform it for the day.

AMRAP- AMRAP stands for as many repetitions as possible.

Chipper- Chipper stands for a workout that involves many repetitions and movements.

PB - personal best.

There are many other such terms that you have to acquaint yourself with in order to use the cross fit lingo.

Here are some of the most widely used workouts in cross fit.

Barbara

5 rounds of

- 20 pull up
- 30 push up
- 40 sit up
- 50 air squat
- Run 1 mile

You have to do all of this within a set period of time and then break for a minute or so and then start again. You have to keep this loop going for 5 rounds. If you do get tired then maybe you can take a longer 4th break but not extend the previous ones.

Annie
50 Double-unders
50 Sit-ups
40 Double-unders
40 Sit-ups

30 Double-unders
30 Sit-ups
20 Double-unders
20 Sit-ups
10 Double-unders
10 Sit-ups

This is a bit tougher than the previous type of workout. You have to look at the time that it takes for you to finish this. The earlier you finish it the better. Try to beat your time in order to improve your routine.

Grace

30 Clean and Jerks

Mary
5 Handstand push-ups
10 One-legged squats, alternating
15 Pull-ups

Angie
100 Pull-ups
100 Push-ups
100 Sit-ups
100 Squats

These form the different cross fit training routines that you can consider making part of your work out routines. As you know, training to work with the seals can be extremely demanding and you have to put in efforts to be as physically fit as possible. You must work on your body's basics and build yourself an efficient one that is capable of taking on any challenge that is put its way.

Remember, the going may be tougher for you at the start than it would be for some other people, but everybody has to start somewhere. With dedication, discipline and routine, there is no place you can go but up. The very nature of proper exercise and work out is that it means constant improvement and strengthening of your body. You'll get there soon enough.

CHAPTER 9: SWIMMING TRAINING

As we already know, swimming is a big part of training to be a navy seal. These men spend a majority of their time at sea and it becomes all the more important to be a very strong swimmer. Their unparalleled swimming prowess is crucial in that it is what makes them as adequate as they are for the unique and demanding nature of their missions. Although being able to swim long distances allows SEALs an advantage of being able to deploy offshore without being spotted, this ability also may prove to be a crucial component of survival in dire situations. And not just survival of an individual SEAL's own self, but that of their comrades as well. Unforeseen circumstances may require one to actually carry their teammate along with all their gear and equipment! This clearly illustrates the importance of being a flawless swimmer in the Navy SEALs.

The seals go through rigorous swimming training and it starts at the PST level. The first routine is known as the combat sidestroke. This is an important part of the routine and you must pay special attention to the style that you pick to swim.

The main style to use is the sidestroke without the use of fins. This is a great position to take up as it provides you with maximum agility. However, you can switch it up with free style from time to time.

The combat variation of the sidestroke is overall the most adopted style of swimming in the military. What makes it so desirable is the fact that it allows a steady and prolonged swim while draining less energy from the swimmer. Of course, this is ideal for combat conditions where a soldier or a SEAL is under plenty of gear and must also wield his primary weapon. Besides allowing for better performance, the combat sidestroke also provides the swimmer with a lower profile, reducing the possibility of detection, which is, of course, crucial for special operations.

With the addition of fins, the efficiency of the combat sidestroke is increased even further. Right next to airdrops and boat operations, swimming and diving are the main means of infiltration for the Navy SEALs. Naturally, fins will greatly facilitate these operations in that they allow the swimmer to harness even more power from this already effective swimming style. The fins will take some practice and training to master, but they are a must.

If you are not accustomed to swimming with fins then you should slowly start with it. It is mandatory for you to make use of fins while swimming during seal training. Many find it uncomfortable to use it, as they will not be accustomed to its form and fitting. If you are finding it tough to swim with fins then you must slowly introduce it in. Trying to do too much at once might leave you confused.

Start with the ankles. That is where you will require most of the conditioning. You will have to first train your legs and then move upwards. If you go about it too fast then you run the risk of injuring your ankles. In case you aren't a very strong swimmer or haven't done much swimming in general, it may be a good idea to first commit to working out your legs, including your feet. You will have to bring your A-game to the table because becoming a very strong and reliable swimmer is paramount to making it as a Navy SEAL and living up to the title.

If you are absolutely unsure of how fins need to be used then it is best that you avoid getting into it at all. Leave it till the screening phase where they will train you. It is better than inviting an unnecessary injury and hurting yourself before the big test.

Much like running, swimming training comes in all shapes and sizes, varying in intensity, distance and timing. And also just like with running, different kinds of sessions and exercises work better with different stages of your training. All of their common ground aside, some may argue that swimming is overall a more effective means of getting into shape than running is. This is likely due to the fact that swimming usually incorporates more muscles and provides a more wholesome exercise. Furthermore, swimming can be done in a very wide range of different forms, which can be combined accordingly to give you a full body work out actually. What suits you better is up for you to decide, but becoming proficient in both is unavoidable as far as Navy SEALs are concerned.

There are three swimming styles that you can adopt in order to improve your speed and distance. They are as follows.

Long slow distance

The long slow distance technique is meant to help you build stamina. They will train you to go long distances without getting too tired. This type is mostly undertaken as the first form of training as it provides you with the right form of agility and stamina training. You have to use this technique to swim 1 to 1.25 miles per day. Don't allow it to exceed that limit as you might end up tiring yourself out on a day when you can conserve energy to take up the other styles as well. One good test to check whether you are doing it right is to speak while taking up the practice. If you are able to hold a continuous conversation then it means you are not doing it correctly and need to put in a little more effort. But if you are able to speak only during breaks then you are getting it right. Your focus should be on trying to catch your breath in between the breaks in order to last the course of the practice.

After you have taken the time to build up your swimming endurance, your confidence in water will have risen as well. It is important to be able to swim outside and swim reliably, as opposed to just making your rounds in a pool. After your swimming skill has been hardened and your stamina greatly improved, it is time to work on your raw strength and become able to swim certain distances in a record timing as well as achieving higher speed and mastering a few of the more physically demanding styles.

High intensity

High intensity swimming training is one where you swim continuously for around 20 minutes without breaking. This can sound a bit too tedious but is the basic requirement of high intensity training. However, remember that this form of workout is meant to be demanding and your body should feel the burn consistently. You should avoid tiring yourself out by over doing it. As is with most forms of exercises, your body will feel conditioned and you won't have to put in as much effort towards achieving this feat after a point in time. You can start out with just the 1 set but increase it to 2 or 3 after a while. The main point here is to remain as efficient as possible to finish the entire 20-minute trip.

As you begin to put in more of the 20-minute swimming sets and increase your resilience, it is a good idea also to strive to achieve a greater distance in this time window each time. A human being can only swim so fast, granted, but you may be able to do better than you think initially.

Intervals

The intervals training are pretty unique and meant to help you condition your body for bursts of energy. The intervals training require you to indulge in some high intensity swimming sessions followed by a break. The break should not be too long and just enough to help you catch your breath back. You have to try and maintain a consistent pace and avoid alternating the speeds. That can throw you off a little. You must also get your breathing right in order to last the course. Once you get accustomed to it, you will know to swim in intervals quite successfully.
Remember that there is a certain pace that you have to stick with when it comes to interval swimming. You have to clock your timing and try to beat it with every successive session.

The basic rule to follow here is to have 100-yard intervals, with a recovery period of 2-2 1/2 times the total time that it takes to perform the work interval.

Although it might seem like it is easy for you to take these three styles up, it is important for you to maintain consistency. Try not to tire yourself out too much by adopting just one style. You should look to strike a balance between all three styles.

You can also alternate between strokes as a means of catching a minor break while still swimming. While your body is burning, even the three seconds it takes to change up the strokes can be a valuable resting point.

There are many things that you can do prevent tiring yourself out. One such way is to swim easy strokes in order to compose your body. Once you regain your composure, you can look to improve your form.

CHAPTER 10: RUNNING TRAINING

Running, like swimming, is a big part of navy seal training. You have to focus on both form and effort in order to make the most of your running potential.

Just as in the case of swimming, you have to start practicing running for the PST stage. You will be judged based on many different criteria including the style adopted to run and how agile you can be. As you know, timing is everything and you have to finish on top in order to get noticed. For that, you have to begin training well in advance and avoid skipping any training sessions as each one counts in the long run.

Each style of running has its own benefits and different impact on your health and stamina development. You may be going for greater distances, best timing or running for the sake of intensity, in any case, each of these approaches will train a specific aspect of your overall fitness. Nonetheless, it's important to balance your training between all of them in order to make the most of your running sessions. Here are the different styles of running that you can take up in order to train like a navy seal.

Long slow distance

Long slow distance is probably the best style to adopt if you are interested in building the required stamina to finish a chosen course. As you know, seal take on special missions which require them to run around quite a bit and so, it is vital that you remain as agile as possible and be prepared to run a long distance. Add to it the need to carry heavy ammunition, which will require you to put in a lot more effort towards training your body.

The long slow distance requires you to put in a consistent effort and pick a low to moderate speed. You have to put in efforts to keep your energy levels up so as to last the distance. Often times, people assume that it will be a walk in the park to indulge in long and slow runs. However, this is not true at all and it will require a lot of effort for you to build the right amount of stamina to last such a course. You have to prepare your body in as advance as possible for it by consistently taking up the practice.

The best way to check if you are getting it right is by talking while running. If you are able to hold a conversation well enough then you are probably going too slow. But if you are managing to have the conversations during phrases then you are doing well. Remember to get your breathing right as that can be a crucial part of your training routine. You can easily tire yourself out if you do not focus on your breath intervals. You have to continuously run at a slow and consistent pace for around 40 to 90 minutes in order to effectively train your body for BUD/S running tests.

Breathing is quite possibly the very key to efficient running. In addition to muscle effort, breathing is another thing, which would preclude you from maintaining a conversation during running. This is because you have to focus on and practice it until you get it right, after which it should gradually become a thing of habit. Just as important as food and water, oxygen must be taken in periodically and in the right amounts to supply enough of it to your muscles and keep your body running smoothly and on your feet. A lack of oxygen during any exercise cannot only hinder your efforts towards getting in shape but could easily lead you to faint as well. Your muscles need to be fueled properly if they are to operate at maximum capacity and get stronger as you intensify your exercises.

Continuous high intensity

Continuous high intensity sessions are where you run for around 20 minutes without stopping. This can be extremely demanding and you must try to conserve as much energy as possible in order to finish such a training session. The training should be demanding but must not exhaust you completely. Although this will happen during the first few days of training, your body will gradually get used to it. Continuous high intensity training is possibly the toughest running routine during PST as also BUD/S. So, it is best for you to start with it well in advance and avoid going into it without any prior preparation. There is hardly any time to recover during your continuous high intensity training session and you have to catch a few breaths within a couple of seconds. While doing so, you have to try and jog or walk fast instead of stopping your movement completely. You have to learn how to put your body in "neutral" while still moving, because if you stop completely, it may throw your whole exercise off. Picking up and maintaining a particular tempo is very important in running. This is because your heart and your breathing would have to be brought back up to speed again if you interrupted them suddenly, which puts unnecessary strain on your body.

Intervals

This is a lot like cross fit training. Here, you expose your body to short bursts of high intensity exercises followed by short intervals of breaks. You are supposed to push your body to the brink and then take a break to help it recover. Push again and help recover again. Keep these loops going until you feel like you have pushed your body enough. It isn't necessary to push yourself too far as soon as you begin, especially if you aren't in the greatest of shapes. Wherever you start is okay because this form of training builds up your stamina relatively quick and you'll adapt in no time. Basically, listen to what your body is telling you and pay attention to its reaction, adjust your intervals as well as your breaks accordingly.

Here, the length of the intervals as also the duration of the run will depend entirely on your level of fitness. You have to pick whatever helps you avail the best level of exercise. If you do not possess a high level of fitness then it is best for you to take several small intervals in between your training sessions. You have to gradually work towards improving your time and level of performance. Work hard, but, like I said, pay attention to the way your body behaves under strain. Relative to your previous physical shape, it may require quite some work to achieve the SEAL level of endurance and stamina. Indulge in consistent and regular sessions and give it some time and you will surely get there soon enough.

It is advisable for you to make use of proper running shoes as opposed to boots. Making use of boots can cause you to develop unnecessary injury. You might not be able to adopt the right style and end up injuring your feet. The best thing to do is to consult an expert who will be able to help you find the right running shoes. Although running bare foot is not advisable, you can consider it if you happen to have a condition that worsens owing to wearing shoes. You can also indulge in trial and error to find shoes that work well for you. Once you find them, you can stick with them until such time as you are trained to work with boots. Sometimes it takes a while for not only your body to get used to the intense training but also your feet. In addition to more serious injury, going straight for boots or other uncomfortable and robust footwear can lead to what is likely the worst affliction in existence – blisters. These horrible lumps of pain are known far and wide in all branches of the military and are quite common. During long marches or running sessions, inadequate shoes coupled with skin not hardened enough will almost always lead to blisters, and starting with the best running shoes which fit you perfectly is your best bet if you are to avoid this problem.

CHAPTER 11: YOGA TRAINING

Yoga is great for developing both mental and physical strength. Yoga has been in existence for a long time and continues to be accepted as one of the most preferred alternate work out techniques. Yoga combines the power of both mental alertness and physical capacity to leave you feeling great about your mind and body.

While it has a long history through many civilizations, it appears as though yoga has been making something of a comeback in the past couple of decades. Given its popularity, there are many instructors and fitness centers around that offer group or individual sessions in this form of training. While those programs can prove useful for a more committed approach to yoga exercise, you can learn a thing or two on your own and see what the fuss is about without straining your wallet. Who knows, you may find that this is exactly the type of thing you need. Many people, from all walks of life, report that yoga has had a tremendous positive impact on their lives.

There are many yoga poses to choose from and each one will have a significant impact on a particular part of your body. Depending on where you think most work is required, you can pick from the routines. Here is looking at poses that are meant to train both your mind and body.

Breathing exercises

Though it is seldom given much thought, breathing holds the key to much more than just keeping you alive. It may seem redundant to point it out, but breathing, or more precisely oxygen, plays a vital role in our daily functioning. This isn't only because it is necessary for survival, but because practicing your breathing and getting it right will have other crucial benefits towards your general well-being and spiritual state.

Breathing exercises are typically meant to help you relax your mind and reel in a sense of calm. There are many breathing exercises to pick from and they are as follows.

Anulom Vilom

Anulom Vilom is a form of breathing exercise where you calm your mind down. Start by picking a relaxing position. Now close your eyes and delve deep into your mind. Place your right thumb over your right nostril and draw in a deep breath through your left. Hold on to the breath and quickly close your left nostril with your index finger while releasing your right. Exhale through your right nostril. Now inhale through your right and close it while releasing the left to exhale through it. Keep this going until you feel light. You can do this for 5 to 10 minutes.

Kapalbhati

Kapalbhati is easy to perform and quite helpful. Start by sitting on the ground and fold in your legs. Maintain a straight back and close your eyes. Now exhale loudly in short bursts. You must swiftly inhale within the gap provided by the exhales. Kapalbhati also has the capacity of helping you trim down your stomach. The physical movement caused by the breath helps in flattening out the muscles.

Bhrastrika pranayama

Bhrastrika pranayama is an advanced breathing technique. It will leave you feeling light and energetic. Start by drawing in deep breaths and relaxing your mind and body. Now close your eyes and swoon down a little to inhale and then raise your head up to exhale. Swoon again; rise again. Keep this going until you feel fully relaxed. You should do this for no more than 2 minutes as it can leave you feeling dizzy.

These form the different breathing exercises that you can take up to relax your mind. Conduct these exercises during your leisure time or in between work out sessions. They will further your ability to relax and maintain a calm composure in daily life while also having an effect on your physical shape. Yoga is a great way to compliment your exercises and training, a sort of a cherry on top.

Tree pose

The tree pose is meant to help you increase your body's balance. As you know, it is important to remain steady in any given position, especially on one foot. Many people fail to do so, which can end up looking quite embarrassing. So, the best thing to do is to practice the tree pose in order to maintain a steady balance. Start by standing straight with your arms by your side. Now look straight ahead and lift your right foot with both your hands. Place it on your left inner thigh. Remain as steady and balanced as possible. Slowly lift your hands above your head and join them on top. This pose is quite tough to maintain, as you will feel like tumbling over. But you have to stay as stable as possible. Remain that way for a couple of minutes before switching foot. The tree pose is great for your back as well.

Remember, it's not only about not embarrassing yourself, having a well-developed balance will help you achieve a firmer grip on your own body. As we have learned already, being nimble and dexterous is an important goal in the course of your training. Being strong and fit is important, yes, but yoga is where you learn the art of calm. It is the way towards assuming control of that strength and of yourself, making your physical power fully work for you.

Cobra pose

The cobra pose is simple yet quite effective in helping you strengthen and tone your abs. Start by lying face down on the floor. Now stare at the distance. Slowly place your hands next to you and lift your upper torso upwards. You shouldn't strain your neck too much though and don't push it too far back. Remain in the pose for a couple of minutes and then lower your upper body down. Lift again and try to curve your body a little. Hold again and release again. Keep this up for a few minutes.

This exercise does wonders for your back as well. Something similar is prescribed by physicians or more precisely physiotherapists, to those suffering from back problems. The cobra pose may be a good way to compensate if your day job is such that it entails a lot of sitting, which a lot of jobs nowadays do.

Triangle pose

To perform the triangle pose start by standing straight with your hands by your side. Draw in deep breaths and look ahead. Now bend to the right to place your left palm next to your right foot. Your body must resemble a triangle when you do so. You must remain in the pose for some time before lifting yourself up. Now bend to the left and place your right palm next to your left foot. Keep doing this until you feel relaxed and fresh.

The triangle pose provides a rather holistic exercise for your body. It activates almost all parts of it and is particularly beneficial towards your arms, legs, hips and shoulders. Consider whether you have recently had any injuries in the aforementioned areas and limbs as the pose also puts quite a pressure on them.

Shoulder stand pose

The shoulder stand pose is a very relaxing pose. Start by lying flat on the ground face up. Now slowly lift your legs in the air. Support your lower back with your palms in order to raise your legs higher. Your upper body should entirely be supported by your shoulders alone. This basically means that your body below your shoulders will now be raised into the air, upside down, with your legs reaching far up and as straight as you can get them to be.

You will find this pose very relaxing as it has been found to alleviate a lot of stress. It also offers some physical benefits to your body, such as helping your digestive system and strengthening those parts of the body, which are raised up, and especially the shoulders. What's more, it is a very basic and simple pose, which anybody can easily achieve.

Plough pose

Plough pose is a little tough to perform but overall a great choice. Start by lying on the floor face up. Draw in a few deep breaths and relax your body. Now lift your legs in the air and point your toes to the sky. Support your lower back with your hands and push your feet backwards. Keep pushing them back until your toes touch the floor behind you. Keep your feet there for a couple of minutes and then bring them back up in the air. Remain as steady as possible. Now slowly lift your feet back in the air and lower it to the floor touching your heels to the ground. Relax your body completely. You can repeat if you like.

Most of the yoga exercises can be repeated as many times as you feel like. Their purpose is to relax you by releasing stress as well as to consolidate your fitness. The important thing is to keep breathing and take it slow, take heed not to hurt yourself by falling or keeling over during some of them, especially amid the exercises which require balance.

Bow pose

Bow pose can be a little tough to perform but one that provides your body with great benefits. Start by sleeping face down on the floor. Now lift your upper torso by pushing it upwards using your hands and lean your legs in towards your butt. Hold your ankles using your palms and pull it further in. simultaneously push your head backwards and try to place the bottom of your feet on top of your head. Maintain this pose for a couple of seconds before releasing. Assume the pose once again and keep going until you feel a proper stretch in your back.

Fish pose

Sit on the floor with your legs stretched out in front of you. Now lie on your back and support your upper body by tilting your head backwards and placing the top on the ground. This might feel a little difficult at first but will get better with time. Bend your legs a little to place your feet flat on the ground and place your palms on your stomach. Remain in the pose for some time before going back to neutral.

Forward bend

The forward bend is an easy one to take up and will help you stretch your spine completely. Start by sitting on the floor and spread your legs out in front of you. Now bend down and try to touch your toes. This might feel a little tight in your hamstrings but will get easier as you go. Doing this often will help you loosen your leg muscles thereby helping you run faster!

Downward dog pose

The downward dog pose is also great for you. Start by standing straight and looking straight ahead. Now bend forward and place your palms on the floor in front of you. Create an arch shape with your body. Push your head down and lift your right leg up in the air. Remain in the pose for a few seconds. Now lift your left leg in the air and remain in the pose for a few seconds. Keep alternating this way until you feel a through stretch in your back muscles.

Child pose

The child pose is also known as Balasan. This is meant to help you relax your body and absorb the effects of the different poses. Start by sitting on the floor with your legs folded under your body. Seeing as your knees will represent the foundation of this pose, it should be avoided if yours are injured. Other than that, this is a fairly basic pose which serves are a filler of sorts. It is aimed at maintaining your composure while at the same time taking a break between the more demanding exercises.

These form the different yoga poses that you can take up and exploit. It is, however, not limited to just these and there are many more that you can look into. It is a well-established and developed practice that has been constructed upon the exercises found in many different parts of the world. To broaden your horizons and gain a deeper insight into what yoga can offer you, commit some time to doing quality research or seek the help of professional instructors.

CHAPTER 12: MEDITATION BASICS

About as long as the notion of spirituality itself, meditation has been around as a central practice within human spiritual and even physical development in many cultures throughout history. In its most elemental and narrow meaning, meditation is really the practice of exercising one's mind. While meditation has almost exclusively been closely tied to religious life and practice, its application stretched far beyond that over the centuries, and especially so in the modern world.

The earliest records of people, primarily monks and other spiritually committed individuals from the religious ranks, predate Christianity by at least a couple of centuries and originate from the Hindu religion. As time went by, various forms of meditations have also weaved their way into the warrior communities in many cultures. Training the mind to have inexorable focus, defeat fear and achieve absolute calm before battle are some of the ends to which meditation has been used. In our daily lives, the battles have changed dramatically, but the state of mind that prevails and successfully navigates the hardships of life has not. As we have already learned, physical prowess is only half the formula; it is your mind that must be sharpened and disciplined to drive your physical efforts.

Chanting meditation

This is the easiest form of meditation that you can take up and yet the most effective. You can start by sitting in a comfortable position and close your eyes. Now draw in deep breaths and relax your body. Pick a comfortable word that you would like to chat like "om". Start by chanting the word in your mind. Then slowly bring it to your lips. You should feel the vibrations all over your body. It should ripple through your body and help you relax. You can do this for 15 to 20 minutes or more if you like. The key is to remain as absorbed in the activity as possible in order to enhance your positive uptake.

Chanting a particular mantra to aid your meditation is an age-old practice originating mostly from religious rituals in Eastern cultures. However, in some form or another, various kinds of chanting have found their way into most of the world's religions down through the centuries. The key here is to harness the power of the human voice and direct it towards inducing a strong sense of serenity. Church liturgies, or even Muslim prayers, make use of chanting in their own way as well.

This, or any other techniques for that matter, will hardly work if you don't bring in the necessary concentration and ensure a peaceful environment. Interruptions and distractions will make it impossible for you to get the most out of your meditation sessions. Meditation needs to be your secure refuge from the daily onslaught of stress. As a matter of fact, having your sessions interrupted may lead to even more frustration and detriment to your overall composure.

Mindfulness meditation

Mindfulness meditation is the next activity that you can take up. It involves remaining seated in a steady position and remaining completely aware of your surroundings. Mindfulness helps in eliminating unnecessary stress and anxiety. Pick a nice spot for yourself like a balcony or your garden. Have an object placed in front of you like a pot or a statue. Stare at it until such time as your mind eliminates all other thoughts and remains fixated on the object alone. Stare at it for 15 to 20 minutes and then draw in deep breaths.

As you might have guessed, the nature of the object itself is irrelevant for the most part. This technique serves to train your level of focus and concentration, your ability to trim away random and interfering thoughts from your mind. Focusing hard on an object and on that object only, no matter how random it may be, may prove to be more complicated than you thought it would be, and if that's the case, then you know why you need to conduct this practice. Exercising your concentration and mindfulness can also help you not think about stressful issues and take your mind off of your problems for at least a while, which has a great therapeutic effect.

Cleansing meditation

Cleansing meditation helps you cleanse your imaginary wheels. These wheels are placed in the center of your body and each one corresponds to a set of organs that they lie next to. By channeling your feminine power you can eliminate unnecessary stress and tensions that have built up in your mind. There are 7 wheels in all and each one lies at a particular distance from each other. The first one lies at the very bottom behind your pubic bone and deals with you being grounded. The second lies below your stomach, the third under your sternum, the fourth next to your heart, the fifth inside your throat, the sixth between your eyebrows and the last one inside your mind. You can stimulate all of these together. Start by imagining a small ball of white light originating from your first wheel and then moving up to the second, then the third, then the fourth, the fifth, sixth and finally the seventh before leaving your body through your head. This will help you cleanse your systems.

Otherwise referred to as chakras, these points in the human body have been believed to hold the key to inner strength and general wellbeing of human beings in many Eastern cultures. They are viewed as sort of map that charts the way to the very spirit within us. These theories persist to this day in that part of the world despite science's numerous gains through the centuries. Meditation's positive impact on our minds and feelings has been directly observed many times. Whether the benefits of these exercises end there or hold much more meaning than we know is something you would best find out for yourself.

Qi gong

Qi gong is a variation of the previous form of meditation. It is suitable for all those that don't have the patience to take up kundalini meditation. Qi gong starts out the same way, by you imagining a small ball of light originating in your first chakra then moving to your fourth and then to your seventh and then again to your fourth then your first and then your fourth again and so on. The light keeps moving in this type of a loop and cleanses your body and mind. You can do this for 15 to 20 minutes.

Guided visualization

Guided visualization refers to making use of your imagination to attract a desired output. This technique is a proven method to get over an undesirable situation as well. To perform this meditation, start by finding a quiet place and lying down. Now visualize yourself in the future and how everything is working great for you. You are sitting in a forest or floating on a river or walking up a golden staircase etc. All your stress and tension has left you and you are feeling extremely calm and relaxed. Your life is back on track and you are feeling extremely delighted. You are sure that everything will now fix itself and your life will improve through several folds. Think of this situation for 15 to 20 minutes or more if you have the time for it. If you have an illness, then imagine yourself in the future where the illness has left you.

Granted, your sheer power of will, may not directly affect the physical nature of your life and the world, but it will affect you. The importance of this kind of thinking is undeniable when you consider that it is you, and you only, who has an actual effect on your life and the courses you take. If your mind is in an inexorable drive to succeed and come out on top, then you most likely will. Many advocates of this practice often stress the power of auto-suggestion, and it's true, auto-suggestion will help you achieve your goals in that it will consolidate the main factor of success – you.

Heart rhythm meditation

Heart rhythm meditation refers to making use of your heart's rhythm to reel in a sense of calm and instill peace in your mind. To perform this meditation, start by sitting in a comfortable position. Now draw in deep breaths and close your eyes. Place your right hand over your heart and feel the heartbeat moving through your hand to the rest of your body. The heartbeat helps in carrying fresh blood to the various parts of your body and enriches your organs. You feel deeply connected with your body and your mind relates to your body's impulses. Do this for 15 to 20 minutes.

Remember to maintain firm control over your breathing. Well-distributed and consistent breathing directly calms down your heart and brings its beats in order. This is why breathing is always advised in stressful situations where panic is a likely threat.

Hypnosis meditation

Hypnosis meditation is a type of meditation that helps you tap into your inner mind to see what lies within it. Most of our dominant thoughts lie in our subconscious mind, which we need to understand in order to exploit our potential to the fullest. You can either self-induce a trance or get someone to do it. If you are doing it by yourself then find a comfortable place to lie down. Next, close your eyes and allow your mind to travel to the back of your head. You will find something there that is not part of your conscious mind. Try bringing it to the front of your mind and ponder over it. Once done, you can slowly come out of the trance.

Frequently done in psychiatry, hypnosis is utilized in order to access repressed memories. This can be done either to uncover mysteries of the past and deal with emotional problems head-on or it can be used to access pleasant memories we may have forgotten. Memories and other aspects of your personality are all registered and stored deep inside your brain. None of it quite disappears from a healthy and functioning brain. It is merely a matter of unlocking these areas and bringing their contents to the forefront of your conscious mind where they can be experienced and contemplated again. In addition to potentially teaching you interesting things about yourself, hypnosis also serves just to strengthen your control over your own mind even further.

Walking meditation

Meditation need not always pertain to an activity that takes place in a seated position alone. There are many types of activity based meditational practices as well such as walking and Zazen meditation. Walking meditation is easy to perform and will help you relax your mind and provide your body with some exercise. To perform this meditation start by finding a walkway that is long enough for you to walk for 5 minutes. Now start by standing straight and your hands by your side. Place your left leg forward whole inhaling and your right leg forward while exhaling. Keep this going for 15 to 20 minutes.

It may come as some surprise that the mere act of walking can have a very positive impact on your emotional state, especially given the philosophy of our lifestyles in the modern world. But, when you think about it some more you begin to see the logic in this exercise. Synchronizing each breath with a step along the way is an efficient way to bring your physical movements in touch with your most cardinal life processes, exemplified in this case by breathing. This will help you feel more wholesome and composed.

Zazen meditation

Zazen is also a movement-based meditation. Sit with your legs folded under your body. Now stare at something in the distance and start a rocking moment. Rock your body forward and backward in consistent motion. Zazen helps you improve your focus and concentrating abilities. Rock yourself for 10 to 15 minutes before coming to a steady standstill.

These form the different meditational practices that you can take up to enhance your mental make-up. Remember to supplement each of your practices with the right type of ending. You have to allow your mind to relax and your body reel in calm composure. Don't be in a hurry to move to the next activity and try to spend a little time absorbing the positive effects of the activity. Hasting through the process and jumping from one practice to the next would defeat the very purpose of meditation. It's all about taking it slow and contemplating each moment and occurrence in your mind as you engage in your sessions.

CHAPTER 13: MEDITATION ATMOSPHERE

The ambience is something that significantly affects our state of mind whatever we may do or wherever we may be. Some of us have more of a nose for these things, but everybody is influenced by the mood around them to some extent. Of course, unpleasant or otherwise disconcerting surroundings severely affect our ability to focus and attain a calm composure.

When it comes to taking up meditational practices, it is best for you to get into the right mood and frame of mind. Meditation is meant to help you reel in a sense of calm and allow you to focus your mind on the various activities. For that, it is best for you to first set the right mood before taking up the practice. Here are some things that you can do towards setting the correct mood.

Atmosphere

You should focus on the atmosphere of the room. The atmosphere should be conducive in order to help you concentrate on your practice. There should be enough cross ventilation in your room in order to help you avail fresh air. Open up the windows and doors. You can turn on the fan as well. If it is too hot then consider switching on the air conditioner. If it is too cold then wrap yourself up to prevent the cold from affecting your practice.

The goal is to ensure that the physical world has as little noticeable effect on you as possible. What you want here is to eliminate outside influence and achieve a full focus on the inner workings of your body and mind. Always take the time to establish the perfect conditions for your meditation sessions. The whole point of meditating is to take your time and get it right; there is no need to rush anything, as this will render your efforts pointless.

Lighting

Focus on the lighting next. The room needs to be ideally lit so that you don't get bored or fall asleep. Don't make it too bright or too dingy. Choose something that lies in between. Picking red or yellow light is great to help you set the right mood. Try using some red, pink or green as well as they too can help you set the right mood for meditation. Lights that are in the form of lamps will work better as compared to overhead lights.

Being that it is one of the main makers of indoors ambience anywhere, from homes to public establishments, lighting should not be overlooked amid meditation. After all, we give it much thought when conducting other leisure activities we care about, think about it. Many of us pay attention to lighting when creating a romantic atmosphere or enjoying a special meal. We also can be drawn to or deterred from a restaurant or pub depending on the lighting there. It's only natural that it plays an important role in a mood-altering practice that is meditation.

Aromatherapy

Making use of aromatherapy can also greatly help you set the right mood for yourself. Aromatherapy has the capacity to help you relax your mind and body. Choose something on the lines of rose or vanilla as both these can help you relax your mind and senses. Aromatherapy aids in improving your overall mood and makes your mind alert. You can consider burning incense sticks or aromatherapy candles. You can also use pot Pourri or cotton balls dipped in aromatherapy oils to place all around your meditation room.

Our olfactory perception of our surroundings has enormous potential to ruin as well as improve our state of mind and even emotions. The scent is something that not only has an effect on us at a given moment but also has the capacity to ingrain itself deeply into our memory. Certain scents we remember will usually tie themselves to particular events or even states of mind we experienced while the scent in question was present. Smelling something we recall from before can trigger very pleasant feelings and memories from happier or simpler times; if you know a few of these examples within yourself it may be possible to use this to the advantage of your meditation as well.

Sound

Sound too can help you relax. Playing a melodious tune can help you generate the right mood. Pick something that has the capacity to relax your mind instantly. If you are used to listening to something calming then use the same. Making use of instrumental music can help you relax better. You can either play a cd or play it through YouTube. As long as it helps you in remaining put with the practice, you can play whatever pleases you.

Many people find classical pieces of music to be the most relaxing and inspiring, but this is not a rule, of course. Different people will find different music soothing and helpful for their concentration. Some may like jazz, others would prefer something more flat, and some of them may even find heavy metal to be calming, but I doubt that one. Either way, this can be a good excuse to discover some new music. While you're committing to your meditation, it could follow suit well to research some eastern melodies of which plenty are very traditional and pristine.

Singing bowls

You can consider making use of singing bowls. Singing bowls refer to metallic deep-mouthed bowls that produce an interesting tune when stimulated. This tune, or tone, helps you relax your mind and body. Singing bowls have existed since time immemorial and continue to be used in many parts of the world. These mystic instruments are widely believed to have originated in Tibet. Although they have found their way to many places around the world, very little is known about their beginnings, or rather about the details concerning their original purpose. This is mostly due to the communist occupation and oppression, which began during the '50s and destroyed much of the deeply religious and spiritual heritage of Tibet.

These singing bowls aid in creating vibrations that is capable of moving through your mind and body while instilling peace and tranquility. You will be supplied with a mallet that you can use to hit on the mouth of the singing bowl to generate the sound. Singing bowls are available in several materials including steel, brass, gold etc. and you can pick the one that you think works best for you.

Idols

You can also consider using idols. You can place these idols in your room and meditate in front of it. You can choose any idol that you think works well for you. Some prefer to have Buddha while others like lord Ganesha. That choice is entirely yours and if you don't want to have idols then you can consider using posters.

It doesn't have to be a religious thing at all. Using idols may simply add to the atmosphere and consolidate the element you are in. After all, aesthetics are one of the main ingredients of any ambience. Furthermore, if you are exercising your mindfulness, focus, and concentration, idols may prove to be an agreeable object on which to center your thoughts. Granted that these objects can mostly be random and of no direct relevance to the practice like I said. However, using one that pertains to the spiritual exercise you are trying to master definitely has its benefits. Contemplating an idol of a particular culture or religion may provide a lot of food for thought and further immerse you into the ritual.

Quotes

Making use of quotes can also help you remain inspired. Choose a nice quote that will help you remain focused. Print it out on paper and make a poster out of it. Place the poster on a wall in your meditation room. Look at it before starting or ending a practice. The quote should keep you inspired and put in your best efforts. Try to accompany with your own inspirational quote instead of simply borrowing it from the Internet.

Again, quotes are another thing to feed your thoughts and contemplation. When we analyze bits of old wisdom and try to interpret their meaning, our minds will work towards these answers, taking all kinds of paths along the way. This may not be the best course to take when you are exercising your ability to concentrate and empty your mind, but drifting away to faraway places in your mind will often prove to be very relaxing.

Distractions

It is important to not have too many distractions when you wish to indulge in meditation. Try to cut it down to a bare minimum. It is best to have a separate room dedicated to meditation, which nobody but you can access. Tell everybody that the room is specifically meant to help you meditate and is off limits for any other activity. You can also close the door before meditating or make use of a do not disturb sign to cordon off the room.

Although we live in an age of distractions, this doesn't have to be a problem if you are dedicated to your exercise. Make your special meditation chamber off-limits to most electronic devices as well, especially phones. Meditation is all about unplugging yourself from the day-to-day stresses, routines, obligations and responsibilities. To truly make the most of your sessions, you must cast all these things aside during this time. As a matter of fact, you actually want to cast them aside, because you will soon enough begin to see just how beneficial this short period of isolation will be to your overall wellbeing.

Partner

You can consider finding yourself an ideal partner to take up the practice with. The partner can be anyone that you think will help you remain interested in the practice and keep you motivated. Take heed not to partner up with somebody who may interfere with your efforts, though. As I'm sure we all know some people are just detrimental to our peace, calm and quiet. We all know a few such examples, no doubt.

It is understood that SEAL training is meant to be a tough routine where you have to put your body through rigorous practices. However, you also need to focus on calming activities that can help you relax and recoil and meditation is one such great activity to take up.

Periods of meditation and recuperating through mental exercises will actually compliment intense physical training very well. This is understood in many cultures as necessary to maintain a kind of warrior spirit and discipline. Various forms of meditation are commonplace in martial arts like Jiu-jitsu, for example, where short sessions of meditating are conducted prior to and after each stretch of training.

CHAPTER 14: MINDFULNESS TECHNIQUES

In the previous chapter, we looked at the meaning and effects of meditation on a person. We know that it is an activity that you can take up to reel in mental peace. However, meditation is not the only practice that you can take up and can also consider mindfulness. Mindfulness refers to being present in the moment. It is a set of activities that helps you remain present in the current moment and take in as much information from your surroundings as possible.

As you are about to see, this discipline is best practiced through very basic, daily activities to which we don't give much meaning in general. The thing about these activities is that they are more calming than we think. Actions such as doing household or other chores, even brushing your teeth, don't require much focus, but if you pay attention, you'll notice that your focus while conducting them is indeed very high. By training your mind to concentrate on these little things, you will teach your thoughts not to stray, and you will keep them at bay.

This approach to daily life will make sure that you never do things mechanically. Your thoughts will be brought under control, and you will maintain a consistent grip on your brain's processes. This way you will make sure that your mind is not racing in a hundred different directions, but is instead always fully present in all daily situations.

Doing so helps you eliminate unnecessary stress and reel in a sense of calm composure. Mindfulness also assists in improving your tactfulness.

There are many mindfulness activities that you can take up and some are as follows.

Mindful brushing

Start every morning by stretching your body out completely. Next, indulge in mindful brushing. Mindful brushing refers to paying keen attention to your brushing activity in the mornings. This might sound strange but is one of the most therapeutic activities that you can take up. Start your day by spending sometime brushing your teeth. Observe the trail that the toothpaste leaves behind on the toothbrush. As you brush, visualize each and every single tooth getting cleaned and eliminating plaque and germs. Once done, rinse your mouth and visualize that as well.

You know, when it comes to being mindful, we can actually learn a lot from children. Sure, kids are usually running around doing a million different things per minute; jumping, playing, fighting, falling. And yet, despite all their hyperactivity, children can get interested in virtually anything, even become fascinated by it. This is gradually changing, but only a decade ago it was all but common to see a child sitting in the dirt and playing with a couple of rocks and sticks, having the time of his life while at it! And much like playing, kids often seem to enjoy short tasks, or at least appear very focused while doing them.

What these exercises are really about is trying to get back in touch with that child within who could stop and stare at anything, no matter how normal or commonplace it is, and contemplate it from all sides, ask questions and wonder about it. Apparently this is something most of us lose as the years go by, but then again, many have managed to achieve it again.

Mindful bathing

Mindful bathing is almost the same as mindful brushing. Here, you focus on the activity of bathing as opposed to brushing. In mindful bathing, you immerse yourself in the activity and shut everything else out. Doing so will help you relax as also heighten your senses. Start by picking a convenient time slot to carry out the activity. Now get into the shower and stand under it visualizing a waterfall. Pick an interesting smelling soap to set the right mood. Start by taking a long deep whiff of the soap and then rub it over your body. Stare at the bar as it leaves behind a trail on your hand. Do the same with the rest of the body. Try spending at least 20 to 30 minutes in the shower instead of rushing out within a few minutes. You have to relax your mind and body. Mindfulness bathing aids in igniting your senses as well and can effectively relax your mind.

Another thing that this frame of mind will help you achieve is an appreciation for the little, pleasant things in life. By taking the time to contemplate and actually enjoy the basic luxuries such as bathing, you will surely begin to see that you have it better than you may have thought. It is very beneficial to remind yourself of just how good these little things are. By doing so, one begins to enjoy life more, while paying less heed to the daily onslaught of stress and nuisance.

Mindful cooking

We already looked at the strict diet that a SEAL has to follow and the foods that are generally prescribed. Using the same, you have to indulge in some mindful cooking. Mindful cooking refers to spending sometime in the kitchen and cooking a hearty meal. There is no point in rushing the process in a bid to get done at the earliest. You have to put your heart into everything that you do in order to avail its true and full benefits. You can get your partner to help out in the kitchen if you wish to save on time. You can also pack yourself a hearty and healthy meal to carry to office.

Don't forget how crucial of a role nutrition plays in training and healthy living. Keep in mind how we said that your eating habits and schedules are the cornerstone of success. Being as important as food is, it is never a waste of time to put in the extra effort when making yourself a meal. What's more, approach it as a hobby or even get creative when you are cooking. Who knows, you may find that you really enjoy making food, as a lot of people do.

Mindful eating

Once the meal is ready, you have to indulge in mindful eating. Take your time while having a meal and don't rush anything. Sit at the table and don't be on the move. Get rid of all the distractions around you and have just the meal in front of you. Take small bites and don't end up filling your mouth with a lot of food. Remain mindful when you pick up the morsel of food and direct it into your mouth. Chew your food down and enjoy every minute of it. Try understanding all the flavors that exist in it and enjoy a thoroughly hearty meal.

You may never stop and think about it, but eating is one of the most important things in life. It's strange how rarely we consider this, given that it is so obvious from a biological point of view. Either way, it is one important thing that can also be a source of utmost enjoyment. After you establish a healthy habit and schedule for your food intake and begin putting in the time to prepare quality meals, it is a good idea to form a sort of ritual around each daily meal. Some people don't like rituals and routine, but taking the time and thought to focus on that which you eat, appreciating its flavor is certainly something we can all do. You will soon learn that respected food tastes the best.

Mindful chores

You can remain mindful while fulfilling your daily chores. These can refer to everyday routine activities that you take up such as cleaning, ironing, de-cluttering etc. Put a check on all the distractions around you and indulge in some cleaning activities where you remain thoroughly mindful of the situations around you. Indulging in Mindful chores aids in eliminating unnecessary delaying and helps you remain calm and composed. Pick an activity and pursue it wholeheartedly until you feel fully satisfied.

And if it's a chore you hate doing, paying some mind to it and analyzing it will not only practice your concentration and composition but may reveal some fun aspects of it. The right frame of mind can make almost anything interesting. A tad of creativity goes a long way in this regard, as does imagination.

Mindful exercise
The next activity to take up is mindful exercising. This refers to paying key attention to your exercise routine as you perform it. We already looked at the different routines that SEALs take up and when you perform these, you have to remain as mindful as possible. But remaining mindful does not mean you cheat on the routine. You have to put in just as much effort while remaining as mindful of the situation as possible. Even if you are tired, don't focus on that aspect and focus your concentration on the routine.

This kind of thinking will also bring you closer to being able to ignore exhaustion as much as possible, which can be pivotal in certain situations. Nature's way of pushing you above and beyond in times of dire need is adrenaline, but you would do well to train your mind to be capable of achieving that extra push on its own. Focusing on the task at hand instead of its consequence on your body will teach you to take the strain and even endure more pain. After all, pain is recognized in your brain in the first place, and it's all about fighting it where it lives.

Mindful listening
The next activity refers to mindful listening. Mindful listening has several benefits. You can use it to relax your mind, increase your concentrations, prepare yourself for something big like a meeting or presentation etc. Before partaking in any of these, start by picking a calming song and give it a good listen. Try to identify all the different aspects of it and the various notes. Divert all your attention to the music and stay focused on it. You will feel relaxed and ready to on the next challenge.

Giving the music a harder listen will be easier and even more beneficial if you are already a music person. Some people enjoy and crave music more than others, but that's okay since virtually anybody has at least a modicum of positive reaction to specific notes, it is rooted deep in our DNA. Find the sounds that relax and otherwise positively impact your mind, and pay attention when you listen. Take the music apart, analyze or interpret it if possible, it can unveil a whole new world you never noticed before. Listening to music can be much more than just mere relaxation it can go as far as being a learning experience.

Mindful counting
Mindful counting refers to indulging in some Mindful counting exercises. You can either count down or count up depending on whatever helps you best. Mindful counting has proven benefits on your mind. You can stave of negative thoughts and promote positive ones. Start by finding yourself a quiet corner and start counting backwards or forwards. Once you reach the limit, start over again.

These are some of the different mindfulness exercises that you can take up within a day. The beautiful thing about this practice is that it will not require its own place in your daily schedule. It is essentially a way of augmenting that which you were doing during your day already. What this is about is simply making the most out of everything, drawing benefit wherever possible, at all times. And, as you can see, virtually any segment of your life can be utilized towards self-improvement and exercise of body and soul. "Live and learn" applies to every single minute of your time on Earth.

CHAPTER 15: GENERAL TIPS

First and foremost, prepare well in advance before the training sessions. As you know, it can be both physically demanding and mentally taxing to take up these routines and it is important that you prepare in both these fields. Don't go into any of the training sessions without knowing what really to expect. You might not be able to put in your best. You have to work out for at least a year before going to the level that these seals go to. If you are someone who averagely exercises and does little to nothing towards maintaining a fit and healthy body then you will find it extremely tough to take up the seal training. Therefore, it is best for you to start training as early as possible.

You will have to work out intensely over that year, mind you. Rising to this level will require both dedication and patience. A strict workout schedule must be established and adhered to without exception. There can be no procrastination, shortcuts or skipping of sessions, as this is unacceptable when exercising on the SEAL level. This kind of routine is a thing of habit and self-discipline because it will require an absolutely consistent approach over a prolonged period of time.

This kind of strict adherence and commitment is problematic for a lot of people, which is why all Special Forces are so few in numbers. Remember well what you learned here so far, the techniques we discussed will help you focus and persevere through any hardship or doubt if you are committed enough. Although it is crucial that you fulfill your end of the deal, there are other factors to consider, factors very relevant to the success of your training.

It is important for you to train with all the right equipment in order to fare well with the training. This includes making use of proper boots or shoes and running consistently. You can also make use of the appropriate swimming wear in order to swim better. Although it can seem a bit tough at the very beginning, it will get progressively simpler and better.

Speed is of utmost importance for a navy seal. Be it running or swimming, you should be able to do both as fast as possible. You can clock your timing when you take up each of these activities and try to outdo yourself each time. Your speed is what will win you all the brownie points and help you do much better than the rest of them. For this, your practice should begin well in advance and you must concentrate on building a tough body that is capable of taking on any kind of physically straining exercises during BUD/S. Mental toughness is of utmost importance when it comes to training successfully for the BUD/s program. You have to indulge in activities that will allow you to remain mentally prepared for any task that comes your way. Mental toughness does not always have to deal with possessing the strength to last the course of the training. It also has to do with being the leader and leading from the front. You have to prepare yourself to gel in with everybody that you come in contact with. This will give you the chance to lead the way for the others to follow suit.

You also must develop a team spirit, as that will go a long way in helping you improve your performance. You will always fare well in a team as opposed to going about it solo. The key is to try and remain as motivated to succeed while being in constant touch with everybody that you rub shoulders with. The test will be just so grueling that there should be no time for any bickering. Try your best to remain as prepared as possible to train with people who come from all walks of life. You have to prepare mentally for it in order to prepare yourself in advance.

It isn't always easy to get along with people, but the Navy SEALs teach their recruits the true value of teamwork and the lengths to which it can take you. As we have seen time and time again, there is virtually no limit to what a well-coordinated, highly functional team of people can accomplish. Learning to work with others and cooperate closely gives you an incredible advantage in life. Everything in life comes easier when you are working with a group and learning this skill is surely a big step towards becoming a more complete and accomplished person, ultimately leading to success.

Remember to keep the time frame in mind when you wish to take up the BUD/s training program. The program can last half a year and you are required to put in tremendous effort towards preparing for it as also partaking in it. It can leave you both physically and mentally tired and you must be prepared for all that comes your way. Depending on your perspective, you may feel that this is a long or short time, but ultimately this doesn't matter. The hell of BUD/S is not a result of the length of the training, but the intensity thereof. Some things in life are hard regardless of the time it takes to accomplish them.

It is important that you undergo regular physical tests to ensure that you have good health. Even if you feel extremely fit, it is important that you have a qualified doctor run the basic tests on you. This will ensure that you avoid unnecessary injuries and can perform quite well during the training sessions.

As long as you are pushing your body to its furthermost limits, you also have to take care of it and keep its health in check. With all its incredible long-term benefits, intense physical exercise can be quite dangerous in some instances as well. This can be due to injury as we have mentioned, but also due to particular health issues depending on the individual. This is why the Navy SEALs always conduct a detailed screening test before beginning the training, and before the following stages of the program. Your body will usually tell you when something is wrong, but this isn't always the case, you may not even realize that the strain you have put on your body has caused a significant problem. Think of it as regular service and diagnostics.

Besides keeping an eye on your health, don't forget what we said about nutrition. The food is the alpha and omega of all fruitful exercise.

Focusing on your diet is extremely important when it comes to excelling in military training. You have to focus on adding to your body food that will allow you to go on auto pilot mode after a while. When that happens, you will have the chance to make Hell Week a little more bearable. The key is to try and develop a food habit that will allow you to increase your body's capacity to take in and burn away the energy within a proper structured time frame. This has to happen over a fixed period of time.

It is always easy to give up but it is important for you to not do so at any cost. You should stop yourself from indulging in negative thoughts that can very well cause you to move away from your motive. As was mentioned earlier, you should remain as mentally tough as possible in order to sail through the seal training. If at any time it gets a little overwhelming, it is best to indulge in an activity that will help you snap back to your normal self.

The temptation to give up will at times be as strong as your determination to make it to the end. This is an autonomous voice that absolutely everyone has in the back of their head, constantly whispering in our ear to yield and call it quits. The trick of all the successful people before us, especially Navy SEALs, is never to let this temptation overcome our desire to succeed. Although the battle of these two forces inside you may at times come to a stalemate, you have to keep pushing and never listen to the insidious voice calling upon you to just throw in the towel. Always back the right horse, which in this case is your dedication and desire to win at all costs. After all, the one you back consistently will come out on top in the end without any doubt.

CHAPTER 16: SEAL TRAINING FAQs

Here are some basic FAQs that need to be addressed in order to successfully train as a navy SEAL.

Is there any typical routine to look forward to as a seal?

No. There is not routine or fixed schedule for a navy seal and they have to prepare to take the day as it comes. The workout that you will be subjected to will vary from day to day. The main activities that the seals need to take on will pertain to physical activities that can be extremely taxing. It is all in a day's work for a seal to run swim and indulge in various other such physically straining activities. A seal is expected to also work in a team and the exercises planned out for each distinct unit will vary.

It's all about being ready to take on the unexpected and about presuming the unpredictable. An established routine allows one to adapt their level of exercise and commitment, often lowering it simply because they know what to expect. This is unacceptable as far as Navy SEALs are concerned. The nature of their missions, as well as combat in general, is such that you must always train hard to be able to surmount any hurdle you may encounter. This is one sure way to be prepared for anything.

How long before I become a SEAL?

It takes around 6 months for a seal to finish all the basic tests and around a year before that to train for the 6 months of training. So effectively, you will have to dedicate around a year and 6 months of your time to become a proper trained seal. This, however, can vary according to the experience and age. If you are looking for proper training to be a real seal then this is the standard time to look at but if you are doing it just to garner confidence in your regular life then the time can be much lesser.

Think of it as a college, which it essentially is in the first place. The world of Navy SEALs is an entirely different one and it is a job that requires a skill set all of its own. The SEALs will make sure you are well versed in these skills and that you possess all the necessary qualities to survive and overcome.

Given the intensity and the amount of learning and agonizing training which occur over this period, don't be fooled into thinking that this year and a half will be over quickly. In fact, this will be the longest year and a half of your life if you embark on this journey.

When did seals come about and why?

Seal teams came about in 1962, when J.F. Kennedy called for special teams to be recruited that would indulge in unconventional warfare. The US navy decided to form navy seal teams 1 and 2. Today, there are around 2,500 seals that undertake extremely specialized jobs like the one that was assigned the Bin laden case.

Although it has been said by Roy Boehm, one of the very founders of the group, that the operational history of the SEALs began in Cuba, the Vietnam War was when this elite unit really came into its own. Fulfilling their purpose of clandestine and anti-guerrilla warfare with great effect, the Navy SEALs earned their stripes in this war and set the mark for decades to come. Michael E. Thornton, Thomas R. Norris, and Joseph R. Kerrey are some of the most distinguished names, all three the recipients of the Medal of Honor!

What is the turnover rate in the seal camp?

Each year, around 1000 navy men take part in the seal-training program to become a bona fide seal. Of these, around 200 make it as seals. This means that around 80% don't make it and only 20% successfully become navy seals. These numbers indicate how grueling it really is to become a seal and how mentally and physically tough one is required to be.

The numbers are there to tell their tale and ensure that nobody underestimates the feat of going for the SEAL trident. They are not to discourage you if you do, in fact, believe that you have what it takes. Remember, the limits of what you can accomplish begin and end with you and you above all.

Can I join the navy to be a seal?

For that you have to consult with your recruiter. If you are above the age of 18 and are interested in joining the seal team then it is best for you to talk with your recruiter about it, as they will be able to better guide you. You might first have to serve in the navy for a while before being inducted into the seal school. But if you are already in the navy then you can consider talking to your command career counsellor who will be able to help you with that decision. You can also call and enquire at the naval special welfare-recruiting directorate to find out.

Will my citizenship matter?

Yes it will. You have to be a proper citizen of the US in order to serve in the navy and become a seal. If your citizenship is pending then you will not have the chance. Similarly, if you hold dual citizenship then you cannot serve with the seals.

Can an army man join the navy seals?

Whether you are in the army or the air force, you should first serve out the remainder of your duty with your specific armed forces before pursuing a career in the navy. After that happens, you can enlist for the navy seal-training program. There are no exceptions here and you should complete the course accordingly.

In other words, yes, any serviceman from any branch of the US military can apply for the Navy SEALs. Depending on your exact position and nature of service, the path towards your application and potential recruitment may differ, but this is something that you can learn easily by consulting those in charge as we already mentioned.

Are there waivers for the ASVAB?

Yes but it is subjective. The waiver will be granted only to those that the authority will deem deserving of one. These waivers are not easily handed out and must be approved by the authorities based on the individual candidate's application.

Is there any set workout regimen for BUD/S?
Yes there is. There is a fixed regimen that you can follow if you wish to take up the BUD/S program. You can download the naval special warfare physical training guide and go through it to understand what you have to do towards training for the BUD/S program. As was mentioned earlier, it is important for you to prepare yourself mentally and physically, as it can be extremely grueling.

If you decide to try for this elite unit, there is pretty much no limit to the amount of training you can do on your own in order to prepare for the hell that is the BUD/S course. The more you exercise and train, the higher your chances of success, and the fact that the Navy provides these regimens to the public is a great help to those interested. Make full use of the available information for the most adequate preparation. Like I said before, you can think of it as applying to college really, a college from hell that is.

What will I need before joining BUD/S?

Nothing. Whatever is required to train at BUD/S will be supplied by the team. You don't really have to buy anything including clothing, equipment etc. If you aren't already used to using fins while swimming then that is something you have to practice before joining BUD/S as you will be required to use it while swimming.

Is scuba diving a compulsory aspect of BUD/S?

Yes, but don't worry, you will be trained in the practice and don't have to already know how to scuba dive. However, if you already happen to know how to scuba dive then well and good and don't have to take up the training during BUD/S. You should expect your skills to be tested, though, as diving is one of the elementary aspects of what the Navy SEALs are all about.

What happens if I don't pass BUD/S?
If you fail to pass BUD/S then you will be reassigned another duty that you will have to take up as a Special Forces candidate. The duty will depend on

your caliber entirely. If you wish to reapply then you will have to wait for 2 years before doing so.

CHAPTER 17: SITUATIONAL AWARENESS

In military circles, situational awareness refers to a person's ability to identify, evaluate and understand crucial elements or information concerning the situations-at-hand that are specific to their missions. Simply put, it's being mindful of what exactly is going on around you.

Navy SEALs, by virtue of their dangerous occupation, value the importance of situational awareness. Without it, there's a pretty good chance that they'll fail in their missions or worse, get killed. While your personal situations may not be as dangerous as those of Navy SEALs, you can still benefit greatly from acquiring the same mindset that they have.

Being mindful and aware of what's going on around you can help you take advantage of many opportunities for promotion, favor, and breakthroughs compared to if you simply coasted through life every day without paying attention. In some situations, a keen sense of situational awareness can actually save your life. For example, many bicycle riders get into accidents simply because they don't pay attention to the road and other motorists on the road as they ride their bikes. Some are even ride bikes while texting on their smart phones with headphones on.

When it comes to winning in the business environment, only those with the keenest sense of awareness about business situations are able to get ahead. It's because successful businessmen have work on being aware of what's going on in their respective markets, industries and businesses. Such awareness allows them to be steps ahead of potentially dangerous developments and hence, continue becoming increasingly profitable. Just ask Mark Zuckerberg, Steve Jobs, Bill Gates, Sergey Brin and Larry Page, all of whom were keenly aware of their respective markets and economies to become billionaires.

While it's true that having a keen sense of situational awareness can be very beneficial, different situations or environments need different levels of such. For example, when you're at home or vacationing at the beach, you should be able to enjoy fully the relative security and peace that such places give you. After all, the reason why you're there is to be able to rest and relax.

On the other hand, there are places like streets, crowded auditoriums, subways or protest rallies wherein you'll need to raise your level of situational awareness to higher levels because these places are riskier then beaches or your home. In places like these, you owe it to yourself and your loved ones to be mentally alert.

Just like Navy SEALs, you can develop your sense of situational awareness by exercising it regularly. How? Regularly, and have fun doing it, assess the places you go to, especially those that you hardly frequent or those that you go to for the first time using the following checklist:

- Try to figure out what the people around you are doing or thinking;
- Try to observe and look for out-of-place things or people who seem to be acting oddly;
- Figure out the best place to seek cover if any unfortunate incidents happen such as gunshots or explosions;
- Figure out the exits nearest you in case you'll need to get out of the venue immediately; and
- Observe if anyone is unusually interested in you (staring, among other things) or is following you around.

As you do this, you will eventually develop the same keen awareness for social, relational, and business situations, which can help you handle them very well like a badass. This is one reason why many ex-Navy SEALs tend to be very good leaders even in the business world. Their keen sense of situational awareness serves them good in practically every area of their lives. You can also benefit from developing a great sense of situational awareness even if you're not a Navy SEAL.

Most SEALs will tell you – a majority of people go through life with little to no awareness of what is actually happening around them. One must be able to identify what is happening around them, then process and comprehend it so that they can react to it accordingly. Of course, you and I *do*, do this on a regular basis; what makes us different from a Navy SEAL who's received training in this area is the time taken to see, process, understand and then react. Civilians like us will end up taking a long time, but in the military, you need split second timing, especially when lives – yours or your teammates' – are depending on your decision-making skills.

So far, we have seen the basic rules of how to become more situationally aware. I must warn you – it won't be easy to get into it! You will need to constantly be on alert; initially, it's very possible that you will end up with horrid headaches and exhaust yourself, given how you are constantly on the lookout for something to happen. However, like with any other skill, the more you practice, the better you get, and the sooner it becomes instinct rather than a conscious thought. And it's that instinct that you want to develop, so that you can react to anything and make a quick decision that could very well mean the difference between life and death.

Remember that you need to react to different environments in different manners. Both your mind and your body require rest, so you need to make sure that you have a couple of places where you can unwind and relax. Home, obviously, is at the top most on this list – it is your best safe house, where you can let your guard down a bit and just let yourself be. However, outside, in crowded places or malls or airports, you must practice your observation skills. We already saw a checklist of things you need to begin following to be able to improve your overall situational awareness.

The simple explanation behind it is that you need to figure out what is beyond the baseline. Let me first define for you what a baseline is.

While the Navy SEALs – and all military units, in fact – have made situation awareness training mandatory, there is a true science behind it, like any other activity, and extensive research has been conducted to try and improve it. When it comes to an extensive training situation like the SEALs, sometimes it's easier to identify what could potentially go wrong in a dangerous situation – in enemy territory, for instance, the SEALs are vigilant for signs of enemy activity, for anything that is out of the ordinary that may cause them harm.

When you transpose that definition into civilian life, things get a lot trickier. What is out of the ordinary? What could cause you harm? What must you be on the lookout for? Obviously, we cannot go around with eyes open for 24 hours in a day; even SEALs need their rest and they take their turns keeping watch. So how do you follow the earlier checklist when you don't even know what you are looking for?

To make things easier to understand, take a look at something called the OODA Loop. This was invented by an Air Force fighter pilot by the name of John Boyd, who also served as a military strategist. He defined OODA as Observe, Orient, Decide and then Act. In any situation, the person who can cycle through this loop fast is the person who has situational awareness.

It goes without saying that most people tend to situation awareness with the first step in the Loop – Observation. This isn't wrong per se, it's just a very limited perception of what the term actually means. The second step – Orient – is where true awareness begins; that is what teaches you how to develop it. Orientation tells you *what* you should be on the lookout for and then helps you put those things into context so that you can react in the appropriate manner.

This why the SEALs are so strong in their awareness of an environment – they know *what* to look for. They know where things could go wrong and they are constantly assessing for threats. This is what you need to incorporate into your life.

So if you take it step by step, the first thing you will need to do is to observe your surroundings, which is what I've been describing so far. But here are a few more things to keep in mind when you trying keeping your eyes peeled for threats. Your body language and your stance make a difference; just as you can identify someone shifty from the way they're reacting, you can also give off 'creep' vibes if you don't keep yourself looking calm and relaxed.

When you have a calm demeanor, you do not attract any unwanted attention to yourself. It lets you remain unnoticed, which – in the military, especially – is essential, if one is to escape with one's life. The less threatening you appear, the better. Another reason to stay calm is this – research shows that the more agitated you get, the more our attention span becomes narrow, which means that instead of taking in your entire surrounding, you end up focusing on only a few things at one time. This obviously defeats the purpose of being situationally aware. To keep your attention and focus open to all details, make sure you're calm, relaxed and composed.

One mistake most people make in the observation step is limiting themselves to a visual stimulus only. Observational skills must go beyond just what you can see; make full use of your all your five senses to be aware of your surroundings. For instance, if a chemical gas was to be released through the ventilation system that is colorless, it's the smell that will tell you that something is wrong. *Anything* can be an indicator; sometimes the lack of sound will be a dead giveaway that there is danger around the corner! Keep all your senses fully functioning and use them to identify threats in your vicinity.

To be able to obtain that level of situational awareness, the first thing you need to do is to place yourself in a position of optimal observation. You don't want to be too obvious to other people, but at the same time you want the best position in the vicinity that offers you the best view of everything and everyone. As we saw earlier, you want to first take a note of all the possible exits within the area and make sure you find yourself a spot that offers both optimum visibility as well as easy access to those exit points. The best idea is to put your back to a wall – that way, the fact that you cannot see from the back of your head doesn't make for a nasty surprise and gives you the possibility of making a quick getaway.

As is obvious, this kind of choice is not easily available in most situations. For instance, if you're at a restaurant, you can't always choose your table – you'll have to go with what the table you are given. But you can still be situationally aware; pick the seat that offers you the best view of the room and offers you easier access to the exit.

Now, improving your observational skills is not something that comes easy. Civilian or not, it takes a long time for a person to not only learn this skill but turn it into a definite instinct and a natural way of life. At the SEALs, it becomes a necessity, given that lack of focus or awareness could get them killed. However, in civilian life, it becomes more challenging to learn that skill, which is why you can begin by playing small games that will help you develop better situational awareness. In fact, if you're thinking about joining the military, this is a brilliant place to start!

Play the A-Game – the Awareness Game. In fact, it's an excellent idea to start this out with your kids; it helps them become situationally aware from a very young age, which means that they are instinctually well prepared for threats! It's very easy to play and it will keep them occupied on long journeys or boring situations. Here is how it goes.

Whenever you are outside, make a mental note of whatever you see – the number of people working behind a counter, the hair color of the person in the seat next to you, the clothes the person in front of you is wearing, how many exits there are and where are they located in relation to your position, etc. Obviously, it's difficult to note *everything* at one go, so start small – give yourself a list and then cross it out one by one. When you leave the place, turn to your kids and make a game out of it. The person to remember the most number of details wins!

While you, as an adult, will find it more tiring and difficult to get the hang of, kids will definitely enjoy it! And you end up giving them a good life skill that may just end up saving their lives in the future, so go ahead and try it! It's the most basic step is learning how to observe better and become more situationally aware.

The next step is to orient. This is where the concept of the baseline comes in. as I've been repeating; it isn't enough to simply observe something. You need to know what to look for, how to recognize threats and then put that data into context so that you can react to it. This is where the Orient step comes into play. There are three things in this phase that will help us become more situationally aware. The first is the baseline and the pertaining anomalies for the environment, the second is the mental models of human beings' behavior that we need to keep an eye out for and the final is our actual action in response to these observations.

So again, what is the baseline? In the simplest of terms, it is the most 'normal' situation to exist; it is the status quo. It is the normal reaction or action or situation that people go through every day. For example, if you are sitting in a coffee shop, your baseline will be people ordering coffees, sitting at their tables and reading books or working on their computers, chatting casually with others, etc. If you are at a library, then the baseline of the environment is people sitting quietly at their tables, reading a book or scratching away at their notebooks or even standing at the copy machines to take photocopies of the texts they'd like to read.

A baseline is absolutely essential for you to establish; it is what allows you to spot anomalies. To define what an anomaly is – it is something that either should not happen and does, or something that should happen and does not. To put it simply, it is the thing that does not belong to the situation; in the coffee shop, if a customer were to march up to the owner and start yelling at him, that is an anomaly. Of course, rarely are they so obvious or open – you have to be vigilant enough to recognize even the smallest sign of an anomaly that could indicate threat. This, obviously, comes only with practice.

It goes without saying that the first step in learning to orient yourself is to establish the baseline. However, what is normal behavior for one person may not be normal for another, so how do you go about doing this? Human psyche and psychology are the most unpredictable things in the world, after all. So there are the main questions you must ask yourself to establish the baseline –

- When you step into a new environment, what is the situation that is existent at the time?
- What is the general mood among your vicinity?
- Statistically speaking, what activity would be considered 'normal' in this scenario?
- What is the behavior, people typically exhibit in this situation?

Once you have answered that question, you will have established a baseline. Obviously, it is not a perfect science, but most of the time, you will get it right. With the baseline in place, you can easily identify the anomaly. Just ask yourself this –

- What stands out of the baseline?
- What could cause someone or something to stand out in such a manner?

As you can see, in order to be able to react to an anomaly, you need to do more than just identify its existence. You need to figure out why the anomaly exists in the first place – why is that person acting the way they are or why has the situation become so untenable? If you don't know this case, your reaction will not be something that could potentially fix the situation.

When it comes to identifying potential anomalies in people's behavior, things can get a little bit tricky. You want to be able to identify a potential threat, not get arrested for randomly accusing someone of something they never did. Another thing to keep in mind is that no matter how hard you practice, your brain's attention span is going to be narrow as it is; research proves that there is only so much we can take in at one time. Processing information requires time – Navy SEALs and other officers have undergone such vigorous training that that time is reduced to a fraction of a normal civilian's, but they struggle too.

So to make things easier – there are three particular types of behavior you need to be on the lookout for. These are the general trends of anomalies, but do keep in mind that psychology and human nature are extremely unpredictable – if you want to learn anything at all from the SEALs, let it be that you should be prepared for any situation. Things may not always fall into these categories, but they do largely follow these patterns, so use them as a guideline to help you become more situationally aware.

LOOK FOR DOMINANT BEHAVIOR

As a person living in society, we usually want to get along with our peers and neighbors and the like. This means that we would prefer to act accommodating and give in to our friends because we want to be liked, we want to be accepted. This type of behavior is generally considered to be submissive behavior and you can expect this to be your established baseline for most situations. People are easy going, people want to accommodate one another and people don't really come off as overly hostile or dominant.

Dominant behavior, on the other hand, is something that strikes you as hostile; it is defined as an expression that is taken to be your body's fight response. Someone displaying this type of behavior usually makes gestures that will make them look bigger and appear more threatening. For instance, the person will try to loom over you or intimidate you by drawing to their full height or thrusting their torso out. As you can see, the dominance is more to do with positioning and power than it does with actual physical stature.

Because most people are willing to submit and get along, dominant behavior can be a major anomaly. If someone is pushy or overbearing or is trying to exert power over another person, you will want to take a step back and carefully consider the situation.

This is where the idea of context comes into play – as we saw in the OODA Loop, it's Observe, Orient, Decide and then Act. You need to decide if the anomaly is an actual threat or not. A person displaying dominant behavior definitely deserves more attention than someone else, but you must take the context into account – what is causing that person to behave in such a manner?

Nine times out of ten, you will find that the behavior is justified; a quick talking down will probably fix the situation and bring the person back to their emotional status quo. It is the tenth situation that is dangerous; it is to prevent that situation of danger and violence that you need to be situationally aware in the first place.

Being aware of these human behaviors and their underlying meaning can also be used to your advantage. Of course, I don't mean that you should have an overbearing and aggressive attitude in life, but to carefully consider the fact that most people are willing to yield when pushed. This can come in handy especially in business.

Namely, exerting just the right amount of dominance on a susceptible individual can turn the table around in many situations, especially when unexpected. Dominance can be presented so subtly, in fact, that most will interpret it as basic confidence. And seeing as confidence is, of course, a prerequisite for dominant disposition, you will have mastered this over the course of your training. Remember to keep your dominant side at hand to use it when appropriate, but also, keep it in check and on a tight leash.

LOOK OUT FOR UNCOMFORTABLE BEHAVIOR

Imagine that you are taking the train to work today – look around you to observe how the rest of the passengers are. Nine out of ten passengers will either looked bored or comfortable (provided there are no crowds and the train is traveling smoothly) in their seats, probably looking out of the window or reading a book or listening to music. This is comfortable behavior; it means that they're well situated and their emotional states are nothing to worry about.

However, if a person looks uncomfortable or is unnecessarily distressed – that's the anomaly you need to keep an eye on.

Remember, once again, just because a person is exhibiting anomalous behavior, it doesn't make them a threat. SEALs have it tough; they need to not only identify a potential threat, but also decide if they must move on it. If they're right, they're saving someone's life – if not, they're potentially causing a major accident.

Fortunately, we don't have to do that as civilians. Unlike SEALs who must take out even potential threats, we can afford to wait until the anomaly becomes an actual threat – you never know, maybe that person was so uncomfortable because he was simply late to work!

This is where a clear line is established between situational awareness and plain old paranoia. Becoming paranoid leads not only to dangerous behavior and accidents but also, to deterioration of the mind's state and wellbeing. Prolonged periods of paranoia inflict tremendous stress and damage on the victim, ultimately rendering any joy of life impossible. This exercise is not about presuming danger at all times; it's about practicing and improving your presence in the situation at any given time. Beware not to go too far and become obsessive, approach it as a hobby or a pastime where you primarily look for interesting details while being observant. Remember that it's about mental exercise, not about looking for trouble. If you look for trouble, you will almost certainly find it, and that way lays unnecessary danger.

Research indicates that uncomfortable behavior that a dangerous person would exhibit is quite specific; they will probably keep looking over their shoulder to see what or who is behind them. They will scan their surroundings constantly, particularly because they are expecting a threat.

Of course, such a person could also just be someone like you, trying to be more situationally aware. If you are getting right, you won't be noticeable to him at all – this kind of instinctive awareness takes time and practice, however. You don't see a SEAL openly scouting out a situation – over the course of their training and in the time they spend in the field, it becomes instinct to them. For you, however, it's going to take time, which is why you should be careful and not act rashly. Keep an eye out on the person displaying such behavior and then take it into context before you act.

Also keep in mind that the opposite behavior can also be suspect; in a situation where every person is uncomfortable, if someone is unduly calm and collected, chances are that they are up to no good. Keep an eye on them while you try to fix the chaos.

LOOK OUT FOR INTERESTING BEHAVIOR

Taking off from the previous idea, most people tend to display bored or uninterested behavior in public. They don't really care about what is going on around them and almost never take note of specific interests or people. If someone is paying something special attention in such a situation, you need to keep an eye on them, since they could pose a potential threat.

These three are the most basic common body language clusters that psychologists define as human behavior with reference to situational awareness. Navy SEALs are trained extensively in identifying these behaviors and anything anomalous to them; they know when someone is not following the status quo and move in to take them out before they can become a threat. Marine Combat Profilers offer us a few other behaviors to look out for in civilian situations that could lead to potential danger. These are –

- Shifty Hands – Navy SEALs (and all military personnel, essentially) look for shifty hands on a person as the first obvious sign of discomfort. The first reason ascribed to this practice is that it makes it easier to ensure that the person is not holding a weapon and is not getting ready to attack them. Reason number two is that hands are the most basic indicators of dangerous behavior; a person is up to no good will wring his hands or twiddle his thumbs or do something with them that indicate at danger. For instance, if a person has something on their body they don't want others finding, their instinct will be to touch or pat that part of their body constantly. This is because they want to ensure that the item is still there – it's a rookie move and it's what will get them discovered. This is exactly the type of behavior SEALs and other military men are trained to spot and take out. You can apply it to your normal life; if someone's hands appear shifty, keep an eye on them to make sure they are not up to anything dangerous.
- Acting Natural – Human tendency is to do the opposite of what we are told to do. So if it's acting *natural* that is required of someone, chances are, they will stand out because they're *trying* to act natural. People who 'act natural' will usually end up over exaggerating or under exaggerating their movements. SEALs in Afghanistan, for instance, are trained to look out for 'farmers' trying too hard to be farmers – insurgents generally

act as farmers to collect information on the military men. So if someone is trying too hard to fit in, then chances are they're dangerous – keep an eye on them.

The final phases of the OODA Loop are to decide and act. Obviously, this is easier said than done, given that most of us lack military or even martial arts training. In a tricky situation, you tend to freeze up or not know what to do; chances are, you have very little time to react to what you see, if it really is a dangerous person in front of you. A Navy SEAL may be able to take out this danger with a well-timed and well-placed strike, but you as a civilian will not have the split second decision-making skills! Add to that the fact that the stress of the situation will muddle you up more – what do you do then?!

My answer is going to be a sorry and rather vague one – come up with a plan of action. It sounds very out there, I know, but there is absolutely no way to predict every possible situation and outcome and then come up with a reaction for it. What SEALs do is generally be extremely aware of the things around them; when you walk into a room, scan for potential exits and entrances and also check to see what you can use as a weapon in case of danger. In the hands of a smart person, even something as innocuous as a pen can be a weapon – in emergency, it's not just your physical or martial arts training that matters. Your body is your strength, but so is your mind! Situational awareness will help you keep your wits about you; that way, you can use what you have at your disposal to make a difference to the situation. This is what SEALs are trained to do, on a larger and much more difficult basis.

Here are a few other things that can help you become more situationally aware –

- Learn how to predict events. Obviously, you cannot possibly imagine the outcome of every situation, but statistically speaking, most circumstances will follow a predictable *pattern*. For instance, if people get on to a train, they're going to sit down and wait for their stop. If someone is acting strangely, that's when you need to get suspicious.
- Don't be complacent; even if there seems to be no opposing threat or no reason to worry, you should be on your guard. If a Navy SEAL were to fall asleep while on watch duty, simply because nothing was happening, it might cost him his life or

the life of his comrades. Complacency usually sets in when things are slow or predictable – don't give in to it. Remain constantly vigilant.
- Be very aware of the passage of time. The pace at which your environment changes is influenced by the actions of each person as well as the movement of time itself; be conscious of the fact that time is moving. For instance, if the bus journey is taking longer than usual, you should go on alert – it could mean that there's an accident somewhere because of which there's a traffic jam. You could get down and help in first aid if that was the case! Keep an eye on your watch and be, once again, vigilant.
- Actively prevent exhaustion and fatigue. If you ask a SEAL why he was ever defeated in combat, he will probably tell you that it was due to a combination of factors, not the least of which were the element of surprise and physical fatigue. Your brain requires rest to process any kind of information; if you are overly tired and exhausted, that's when you tend to miss details in your vicinity. A minimum of 5 hours of sleep a day is required to function; the advised number is 8, obviously, but a Navy SEAL cannot afford to always get that much. As a civilian, you have that luxury, so make full use of it – if you want to be constantly vigilant outside and situationally aware, and sleep through the night!

Ultimately situational awareness is about knowing what the status quo is and then identifying something that does not fit into that mold. Despite how much we all want to stand out and be our person, human tendency is to follow the social norm – moralistic implications aside, this sociological aspect is what you need to focus on to become more responsive to potential threats in your environment. Navy SEALs may or may not get the crash course in psychology I just gave you, but these are the concepts they use, nonetheless – they are thrust into situations such as these, where they have no choice but to use their observational and decision making skills. The split second could make the difference between life and death – you, as a civilian can also make that difference by constantly practicing being more aware of your surroundings!

CHAPTER 18: NUTRITION

It's been said that when it comes to physical health and fitness, it's more nutritional than physical. What this means is that what we eat has more impact than how much and hard we exercise.

That's so true. If physical conditioning is the primary way to health and fitness, why is it that many triathletes who don't watch what they eat end up with health issues? I even know of one triathlete friend who suffered a mild stroke while in peak competitive condition, i.e., lean and ripped. It was because despite his lack of body fat and excellent physical shape, his diet was terrible and his cholesterol levels were off the charts.

Consider too that many people who work out at the gym, run every day for miles, and perform thousands of sit-ups and crunches continue to look more like the Michelin Man and the Pillsbury Boy than fit and lean athletes. Why? Chances are, their nutrition is poor, i.e., low in protein and high in sugary and fatty foods.

Given the very demanding nature of their jobs, Navy SEALs need to be in excellent physical and mental shape and health. As such, nutrition is very important to them. And even if you're not a Navy SEAL, nutrition should start becoming very important to you too.

If there is one thing in life to which you can never dedicate too much effort and discipline, it is, indeed, your nutrition. Food is the source of all life, and the quality of your eating will directly dictate the quality of your life as our unfortunate world keeps demonstrating to us throughout the globe. Much like exercise itself, a healthy and well-balanced diet is a thing of habit and schedule for the most part.

While putting in the muscle in the course of your work out is only half the battle, food is the other half. The best way to achieve the perfect eating habit is through basic organization and discipline. Follow the specific guidelines and concoct a daily timeline for all your meals, as well as a variable array of different foods to consume. Adhere strictly to your plan and you will begin to see results within weeks.

NAVY SEAL DIETARY GUIDELINES

Since they operate in many different situations, Navy SEALs use several dietary guidelines. In general, they follow the Navy Operational Fitness and Fueling Series or NOFFS for optimal nutrition and performance. The NOFFS is a nutritional program that limits the consumption of processed foods and instead promotes the consumption of natural, whole foods such as whole grains, veggies and fruits. Further, Navy SEALs are advised to get up to 65 percent of their calories from carbohydrates, up to 30 percent from protein and the rest from fat. This high-carbohydrate, high-protein ratio is designed for fuelling their physically demanding activities as well as muscle maintenance or building.

Diving Dietary Guidelines

Diving and spending extended periods of time underwater can raise some nutritional concerns for Navy SEALs, particularly energy expenditure and dehydration, both of which are heightened underwater. The Navy SEALs' fitness guide suggests the consumption of foods that are high in carbohydrates or carbs like fruits, rice and pasta in between missions and to load up on carbs before a scheduled mission dive. Loading carbs means bumping up carbohydrate consumption by as much as 1,500 extra carb calories while reducing protein and fat consumption three days before a prolonged, scheduled dive.

For hydration, Navy SEALs regularly consume liquids with up to 8% carbs throughout their training sessions or missions to maintain healthy sugar and hydration levels. Another purpose for this hydration technique is to replenish zinc, chromium, magnesium and calcium that are excreted through urination, which is more frequent while in cold water.

Extreme Temperature Dietary Guidelines

Because Navy SEALs also operate in extreme temperatures, their nutritional needs also adapt to such conditions. When operating under extremely hot weather, they ditch excessive protein and fatty foods, both of which tend to make it harder to tolerate heat. They also consume more drinks that are fortified with potassium and sodium, which are rapidly depleted as they sweat excessively in hot conditions and deficiencies of which can increase the risks for muscle cramps.

Under cold conditions, Navy SEALs also limit their consumption of protein and fat because excessive amounts of such can cause dehydration and stomach problems. They also increase consumption of thiamine and other vitamins and minerals essential for energy metabolism. Nuts and whole grains can help augment these nutrients.

High Altitude Dietary Guidelines

Navy SEALs bump up their total calorie consumption when operating on high altitudes because such an environment tends to increase metabolism. It's not unusual to find that on average, SEALs consume up to 6,000 calories daily while operating way up there. Typically, they consume high carb meals for maintaining body weight and energy. They reduce protein intake to 10% at most because more than that, the risk for dehydration is significantly increased.

EATING FREQUENCY AND PORTIONS

For optimal metabolism, they eat smaller but frequent meals. This means they eat 4 to 6 meals a day, every three hours. Doing so helps prevent binge eating and optimal calorie burning. Bodybuilders and fitness experts use the same technique to get lean and ripped – and you can too! Every seen an obese or out of shape active Navy SEAL? Now you know why!

How much should calories of food should each meal contain? According to www.navyfitness.org, the following meal serving portion sizes are highly recommended:

-Carbohydrates – size of the fist;

-Proteins – size of the palm; and

-Dietary Fats – the size of the tip of the thumb.

So how do you employ this kind of a dietary regimen into your daily routine? As is obvious, you will probably not use the dietary guidelines they follow at high altitudes or while diving. You can, of course, try out these activities and follow the set guidelines, but for a day-to-day basis, what you want is the simple, easy to follow diet that you can make part of your daily food and exercise regimen.

Former Navy SEAL, Stew Smith, who now works as a Strength and Conditioning Specialist (CSCS), certified by the National Strength and Conditioning Association, recommends the following the simple diet in his fitness books. The diet has been designed to help you trim the extra fat and get into shape. Do keep in mind – you have to work out and do regular cardio and abdominal exercises if you want it to work! Like I said before, your diet and the actual physical exercise each account for about 50% of the whole process. The more you focus on setting up an efficient eating program, the firmer the base of your work out will become. If your efforts are supported by a strong and healthy diet, there is virtually no limit to how far you can develop your body. Here is how it works –

FIRST MEAL – 6.00 AM – PRE-WORKOUT MEAL

Yes, you start your day off with a meal. The general belief amongst people is that you need to work out on an empty stomach; however, it's better to make sure you have the energy to do your heavy-duty exercise. Plus, this meal is going to give you the fat content you need to function – you will have the whole day to burn that fat off!

What you can take in this meal are these items –

- Try egg white omelets. As I said, you can afford to eat a little bit of fat with this meal, so you can afford to try out a little bit of cheese and pepper to season with. Add some vegetables as

well and a little bit of turkey breast if you are craving some meat. Smith recommends that you keep your Omelet count to not more than 5 eggs for this meal.
- Eat 2 slices of wheat toast. If wheat bread is not available, try out multi grain bagel. Smith claims that he likes to add low fat peanut butter or sugar free jelly – season it with something that is not too fatty and you'll be fine!

Even though you can try to add a little bit of fat for your meals, try to eat as many grains as possible – avoid white breads, pasta and the like. What you need is protein content, with just the right amount of carbs to give you the energy you need, while still fulfilling both your stomach and your taste buds!

Most importantly – work out in the morning! Early morning workouts are absolutely essential; you burn the fat content and you keep yourself extra healthy by taking in the fresh, crisp air of the mornings! You may not be able to gain access to those high altitudes and crisp air that Navy SEALs acquire, but you can definitely set your alarm to a 5.00 o'clock awakening!

Taking on the day after a successful early work out will give you a new perspective; you will find that this activity unlocks a whole new state of mind through which to traverse your day. Instantly, you will begin to feel more confident and fresh as you tackle your daily challenges. Even the basic military branches adopt this technique, let alone Special Forces such as the Navy SEALs. It's all about getting that worm before the other birds.

SECOND MEAL – 9.00 AM – POST-WORKOUT

It is now that you are allowed to eat a bit of carbs – they will help your body in the transport of insulin in your body as well as help you recover from the intensity of your workout. Here is what Smith recommends as food choices for this post workout meal –

- 2 bananas with a glass of milk – choose only skim milk to reduce further fat content.
- Oatmeal with raisins is also a food option – add skim milk to this as well.

If you do not feel like limiting yourself to a single option, mix up smaller portions of both. And if you are still hungry, then add a fruit to your diet – which way your stomach is filled but you keep your body healthy and fit!

Fruits are always welcome so add more of them to your diet whenever you feel that you are craving more food. In almost all cases, you just can't go wrong with fruits; they are a truly benevolent food source.

THIRD MEAL – 12.00 NOON – LUNCH

The third and the fourth meals are probably the trickiest ones for most people; you are at work and you barely have enough time to sit down and eat properly, much less take note of what you can and cannot eat. But do keep in mind that you cannot ignore your nutritional needs – the SEALs have to survive in the wilderness and horrific conditions, despite which they manage to watch what they eat and keep themselves super fit. Make use of the extra time you get when you wake up so early in the morning – pack your own lunch, so that you are not left dependant on the vending machine, that – more often than not – has only unhealthy, greasy options for food. Here is what Smith identifies as good food options for your third meal –

- Ground Turkey Breast – you can add a little bit of cheese, but stay away from the mayo! If you want a little bit of taste, add some mustard or low fat salad dressing and then package the whole item into a wrap made out of whole-wheat grain. You eat as many as 2-3 of these, depending on how hungry you are. A good idea is to throw in some vegetables like bell pepper or tomatoes, since they're quite filling and do not add to the fat content!
- Baked potato chips are something you can use to augment your lunch – keep the quantities small and make sure that they are not fried, only baked.
- Broccoli – don't make that face, broccoli is an excellent and healthy food option for anyone trying to stay fit! Spray a little butter to it if you like; don't use too much though, or you'll add more fat content than you can afford to your diet!
- Fruit – You cannot avoid fruit if you want a healthier diet!

FOURTH MEAL – 3.00 PM – POST-LUNCH MEAL

Again, you want to keep this meal simple and easy, low on fat and carb intake. Here are your food options –

- Try out a can of tuna fish – a single can should go a long way to filling you up!
- Egg whites are also a good idea; augment it with a multi grain or a whole-wheat bagel or bread.

To make it easier to pack your meal in the morning, you could just add another wrap to your noon lunch and eat that at this time. If you do go in for that option, throw in some fat free yogurt as well as a few vegetables – raw ones – like cold carrots to keep your taste buds happy.

Before your next meal, complete go and work out! If you're trying to get fit and into shape, you will need to be determined about your exercise regimen; you have to work out twice a day at least, to be able to condition your body and whip it into shape. While your early morning workout must be intense and powerful, you can try a simpler routine for the evenings, like lifting lightweights or simple calisthenics. Make sure you work out though, no matter how tired or exhausted you are. In fact, the more exhausted you are, the more you need to work out – that is the best way to emulate the SEAL training and learn their grit! Giving up "for the time being" or "just this once" is giving up nonetheless. You cannot afford to skip a single session, not only because it is a slippery slope, but it also detrimental to your routine as a whole. Missing out a work out session or slipping up in the course of your diet, even for one time, can throw your whole effort off and require even harder work to make up for it.

FIFTH MEAL – 5.00 PM – POST-WORKOUT MEAL

You want to keep this meal extremely light, since dinner is just around the corner and you don't want to overstuff yourself. In fact, this meal is more of a quick snack than anything else – it's just to give you that extra energy until dinnertime comes and you can have an actual meal. Here's what you can eat –

- Have a can of tuna once again and make sure you keep your mayo intake as little as possible.

- A small and quick salad, with maybe a single piece of chicken.
- Some wheat crackers to nibble on.

Smith also recommends that you take a protein shake or two after your second workout; however, you should make sure that it is low in fat content. You don't want to regain all those calories that you just lost! Working out so hard, and then just reloading on your fats and calories right after the round is self-sabotage and will surely make you stagnate.

SIXTH MEAL – 6.30 PM – DINNER

This is another meal that you can add carbs to, given that you've completed a workout and require the extra energy. Be very, very careful though – don't confuse carbs with fat! The last thing you need before you head to bed is fat; unlike in the mornings, it doesn't get burnt away. Instead, your body stores it up over the night, adding to those extra pounds! So good carbs are the way to go here! Here is what you can eat now –

- Multigrain pasta is the best option for you at this time! It offers your protein and carbs, with little fat and gives you an enormous amount of energy! You can season the pasta with a good, tasty sauce, but make sure they're not fatty or greasy sauces.
- Augment the pasta with a bit of garlic bread – make sure you use wheat bread for it when you prepare it!
- Turkey or chicken breast, fish or lean steak are also good options, though Smith advises you to add smaller portions of these into the pasta itself, instead of making them whole meals. That way, you get a wonderful array of foods to give you the protein and carbs you need, but it doesn't affect your health adversely!

Head to bed by 10 pm. Give yourself at least 2.5-3 hours for the food to settle in your stomach and start digestion.

As you can very well see, the diet follows the Navy SEAL pattern of eating small but regular and healthy portions! The goal is to eat around 5 to 6 times in one day – all your meals are spaced out at time intervals of three hours. This is because three hours is generally how long it takes for your stomach to digest and empty itself of food. Whether you follow the SEAL pattern or not, every dietician will offer you this piece of advice – never fill your stomach.

I don't mean starve yourself; I mean that you should eat just enough to feel full, not stuffed. This is why the portions are small; it helps boost your metabolism, provided you're exercising regularly and keeping yourself active.

Do not skip meals at any cost; this is when your metabolism slows down and you don't burn as many calories as you would like. Keep your diet rich with protein and a few complex carbs – fat content must be low and preferably negligible! Don't confuse carbs with fat; that's something most people do in their attempt to get fitter. Carbs are something you need, especially after workouts; fats, on the other hand, are better kept at a low minimum – you need them, but at low quantities, so stick to that!

Remember work out – do not skip your exercise regimen, especially since this is what whips your body into shape and conditions you to strong and adverse situations! As you saw, the Navy SEALs undergo the most rigorous, painful physical training you can possibly imagine; obviously, you cannot jump into that kind of physical workout as a civilian and a beginner at that. But you can make sure you complete your exercises; depending on your fitness goals, this can be any type of activity, from fast walking for 30 minutes to a proper sprint for half an hour!

And most importantly, do not forego drinking water during your workouts and the rest of the day! The reason most fad diets and quick weight loss solutions don't really work is because they reduce your muscle mass and water content; it's not *fat* you're burning, it's simply the water in your body that you sweat out. Rehydrate after your sauna session and you'll see that you regain your weight instantly. This is why moderate diet and good exercise are the best ways to lose weight and keep fit – no such thing as easy route to health, I'm afraid!

Drink water before you begin your meals; it fills you up so that you automatically reduce your food content and eat less. Keep in mind that it takes your body about 20 minutes to understand that it is full; so don't keep stuffing yourself even after your designed intake is over. Give yourself those few minutes so that your body knows you're done – you may still have that phantom hunger once you're done eating, but don't give in to it! A good idea is to time your meals – don't listen to your stomach or tongue to eat, listen to your clock so that you're taking timely, small and regular meals that keep your body fit, even if it takes a while for it to feel that way!

Stew Smith's diet plan is an excellent idea for anybody trying to get into shape; you can check out his books for further instructions on how to work out, how to maintain a healthy lifestyle through good food and good exercise. Within the diet itself, he does offer other options too. Here are a few of them –

- A chicken salad that has no fat dressing
- Multi grain pasta, containing turkey, sausage and peppers (preferably the red and yellow ones), dressed with fat free sauces
- A turkey breast burger that is made out of wheat bread
- Roasted chicken breast, with little to no mayo, augmented with honey mustard instead
- For a quick snack, any fruit or vegetable and a pinch of no fat yogurt.

As you can see, options are limited, but you can definitely get creative with your cooking! Just keep your fat content to less than 50 grams or so, and avoid as much processed food as possible to keep yourself healthy and fit!

Apart from your diet and your work out itself, there are some things you need to keep in mind when it comes to getting yourself fit and keeping yourself healthy. Here's what you must do.

CHEW YOUR FOOD WELL

When you put calorie dige4stion with extreme physical activity, your stomach will definitely take a hit. That's probably the reason why you feel so hungry all the time with your extensive workouts and exercises regimens. This is why you need to chew your food – even if you are late and you need to rush off to work, make sure you chew each bite at least 20-25 times.

Chewing initiates the digestive process and helps with nutrient absorption; as you studied in 10th grade biology, digestion begins in the mouth, when you start chewing. So don't just bite or nibble your meals, make sure you chew them properly!

DRINK PLENTY OF WATER

As I already mentioned, water is absolutely essential pre, during and post workouts. You want to make sure that the loss of electrolytes from your body through your sweating doesn't make you faint; water also helps burn excess fat and keeps you hydrated and healthy.

DON'T *WAIT* TO EAT OR DRINK

A big mistake most people make when trying to get into shape is ignoring food and water until they're starving. When you do this, you end up binge eating or taking in extra greasy and fatty foods! The whole point of the aforementioned diet is to eat small, regular meals and stay ahead of your hunger and thirst. You want to make sure that you don't feel hungry or you don't feel extremely full – the status quo is that your stomach is satisfied and isn't growling at you to eat *right* now. It's about evening out your food intake throughout the day for optimal satiety. If you shove too much food into a single meal and cut down on the number of meals you take per day, you will get hungry even though you have already taken in a sufficient amount of calories to get you through the day. Obviously, this leads to overeating and building up unnecessary fat.

DON'T DO HEAVY WORKOUTS ON AN EMPTY STOMACH

As you saw within the diet itself, a pre-workout meal to give you the energy to perform intense exercises is a good idea. Fat loss is something that happens *over* the day and in regular intervals; count your calories and focus on improving your energy levels through the day by eating healthy. If you work out intensely with little to no food in your stomach, chances are your energy levels will dip and you will feel faint and too tired to tackle the day. Instead, eat a healthy, pre-workout meal that will keep you energetic enough to get you through your exercise regimen! Of course, you don't want to just get buffed and fit without feeling healthy at the same time. Balance is key, as it will help you enjoy the fruits of your efforts while, at the same time, feeling as good as ever.

Ultimately, having a good diet and regular work out sessions is absolutely essential to leading a healthy lifestyle. If you want to be more like the SEALs and practice the more intense stuff, try to intensify your workouts to include challenging exercises like diving or mountain climbing or even hiking; these will help you incorporate actual dietary guidelines that the SEALs make use of. But do keep in mind that as a beginner, you may not be ready for these. Start small, work steadily and don't give up – eventually, you will get there!

KEY HIGHLIGHTS

SEALs are some of the toughest people on earth and take up the most arduous tasks on the planet. Right from the navy to army to the air force, these SEALs can be dealt with numerous tasks that require them to be both mentally and physically strong.

Since these SEALs carry out unconventional missions, it is important for them to take up unconventional forms of training as well. The training that these SEALs are exposed to is much more demanding than what regular men in the armed forces have to go through.

Of these SEALs, the ones in the navy possibly have the toughest job owing to the kind of demanding atmosphere that they need to train within. The water bodies that they train in live in can be quite unforgiving and it is important for a SEAL to be available 100% in order to train efficiently.

The training that these SEALs receive can be both mentally and physically demanding. The sessions can be quite rigorous and push the candidate to the very brink.

Why exactly is the Navy SEAL training program so agonizing? What is it that makes their missions so unique, dangerous and important? Well, the key to answering these questions lies within the meaning of unconventional warfare. What makes them stand out from the usual military doctrines is the covert nature of their operations as well as their small numbers, special tactics, and surgical approach to each task.

It's about building tight-knit teams of small size, able to operate deep behind enemy lines before any large-scale operations conducted by conventional and larger military forces. Navy SEALs act as an arrowhead in that they go in first and often cause the most damage! This damage doesn't necessarily have to be manifested by a large body count, massive destruction of enemy forces, etc. No, it's about hitting where it really matters with maximum impact. As a matter of fact, Navy SEALs, and other units with a similar purpose will often turn the very course of the battle in a different direction without the conventional armies on both sides even knowing.

The role that the SEALs played at the beginning of the First Gulf War of 1991 is an excellent example of what these small and elite units can do and how their actions influence the course of battle. Infiltrating themselves into Kuwait City, which was under full Iraqi control at the time, they were the first Coalition boots on the ground. Later on, Navy SEALs carried out a ruse mission to divert the Iraqi military from the main invasion location by detonating explosives and placing markers just off the coast of Kuwait. Ultimately leading the Iraqis to believe that an amphibious attack was underway, this diversion worked and significantly reduced the coordination of Iraqi defenses against the real offensive.

This is how a well-planned and highly strategic move, employing unconventional means and forces, tips the balance of war and potentially saves many lives among the regular military troops. In addition, these men will collect and provide invaluable data on enemy activity as well as rescue hostages and secure American citizens in crisis-stricken areas, all without kicking up any dust.

These are the reasons why Navy SEALs are such a renowned and valued fighting force. This is why so few candidates make the cut and conquer the training course successfully. There is little to no room for error in this line of work, and only the very best will be admitted, regardless of the number of candidates.

There really isn't too much of a restriction on who can and cannot take part in the SEAL training. As long as the candidate is 18 years old and a member of the US navy, he or she (there are talks of women being allowed to join in) can participate in the SEALs training program.

These candidates generally come in big numbers but only a few get the official title of being a SEAL. It can get a bit tough and so, around 70% don't make the cut.

There are basically two training sessions when it comes to being a SEAL. The first involves going through a physical screening test to see if you will be a fit candidate and then training for the next and most important activity, BUD/S.

As many as 90% pass the screening test and are sent to an academy that prepares them for BUD/s. BUD/s is extremely tough and in order to take it up, the candidate has to prepare both mentally and physically for it. The academy is known as special warfare preparatory school and involves going through rigorous tasks to ensure that the candidate is fully prepared to take up BUD/s training.

Take a second and contemplate that yet again. After passing the basic physical screening test, the candidate is sent off to train rigorously and profusely in order to get into the main training course. Consistently growing in difficulty, these segments of training serve as separation layers. Each layer will strike off and weed out a certain number of unfit candidates. This goes on until the very finest men are all that remains, and then it keeps getting worse.

BUD training takes place in three phases with each one being more demanding than the other. The first phase lasts 7 weeks and involves the candidate going through the toughest mental and physical challenges. It involves running constantly for several miles, swimming in extreme conditions, passing through obstacle courses etc. All of this can be extremely demanding and cause the person to tire out easily. However, that is never an option and the SEAL must be prepared to pass through these tests with flying color in order to move to the next phase that is Hell Week.

All the while, the candidates are welcome to quit and put an end to the pain, even during Hell Week. The act of quitting even has a name in the ranks of the Navy SEALs. Commonly referred to as DOR, which stands for "Drop on Request", all a candidate has to do is say the words and then conduct a little piece of tradition. This ritual consists of a surrendering candidate placing his personal headwear next to a specially designated pole that has a bell on it. Finally, ringing the bell three times announces, for all others to hear, that the candidate refuses to go on and is ready to pack up and throw in the towel.

Those who quit and pack up are no Navy SEALs and never could be, at least in their current frame of mind, so the system works like a charm. When you really get down to how it works, you'll see that a SEAL is already there as soon as he steps foot into the training course, while the program serves only to point him out and separate him from the rest.

This testifies further to the fact that it's your mental strength that counts the most. If you are in the training program, that means your physical fitness is already satisfactory at the least, and will naturally come into its own during the course. However, if your will is not hardened, and your determination isn't a thing of steel, you will fail.

Swimming, as you know, is the most important aspect that will be considered at BUD/S. you have to be a strong and prolific swimmer in order to fare well at the BUD/S training. For that, you might have to prepare well in advance and equip yourself with the swimming techniques that are needed to do well. You have to prepare your body to move in harsh conditions and be able to perform well.

Hell Week is the most dreaded time in the SEALs training routine. It pushes the candidate to the absolute extremes and causes almost 50% of them to give up. Hell Week routinely lasts for around 5 days and the candidates are put through extreme physical and mental conditions. They are made to run, swim and take up other grueling physically demanding activities without getting more than 1 hour's rest per day. So in all, they end up getting less than 5 hours sleep and end up feeling absolutely exhausted.

And most of these hellish activities are not meant to make them physically tough but instead mentally. They are meant to help the SEALs develop mental fortitude.

The seals have to follow a particular diet that helps them maintain a strong and lean body. The diet should incorporate foods that are all healthy and nutritious. We looked at the main diet that the seals can follow and you can go through it again if you wish to understand it better.
This book is meant to be an educative platform to help you understand how tough it really is to become a bona fide SEAL. It is

also meant to serve as a handy guide to all those that are interested in training and becoming as tough as a seal. It doesn't really matter from which area of life you come from as long as you wish to become just as tough as these seals. You can consider taking up these exercises in order to get over your inhibitions and improve upon your overall confidence levels.

There are many areas of your life that you can successfully improve upon by choosing to be a seal. These include your level of fitness, your mental structure and also your nutrition. Seal training can make you a whole new person capable of doing a lot of things with much ease.

Apart from this kind of rigorous training, the SEALs can also indulge in meditational practices. As you know, it is extremely important for a navy seal to develop immense courage and confidence in order to finish practice and also serve as a seal. Such mental toughness is not easy to develop and the seal is supposed to possess a lot of mental stamina to be able to complete the tasks and become a seal. The seal is supposed to literally forget about the concept of "fear" and try to develop a strong resistance against it. Fear generally causes people to not put in a 100%, which can work counter productively to the training. The most basic approach that seals take to overcome such fear is put themselves in situations that really do really scare them. Doing so can successfully help in getting used to the fear and chasing it away. Of course this is easier said than done and yet, seals have to mandatorily partake in it to develop mental toughness. A great way to pursue it is by setting reasonable goals and then going about the "facing fear" activities.
These practices are meant to help reel in mental peace and tranquility. We looked at the different meditational practices that you can take up in order to prepare yourself mentally. If you are determined to take up the proper SEAL level practice then it is best that you take up meditation for at least 3 or 4 months leading up to the practice. This will help you mentally prepare for it.

Apart from meditation, you can also consider taking up mindfulness. Mindfulness helps you remain thoroughly aware of your surroundings and put an end to distractions. It makes you mentally and physically strong. Of course you might not be able to compete with the level that these navy men possess but can try and come close to it. Don't think just by meditating and remaining mindful you can successfully finish Hell Week with ease. You will still have to go through the immensely insane physical activities in order to sustain a real SEAL like training.

It is essential for you to undergo regular health check-ups. Many people forgo it thinking they will be fine, but it is best to not take a risk with your health. There will be mandatory health checks that will be issued during BUD/S and you have to strive to maintain clean health. Do not skip meals and continue to push your body until you develop proper immunity.

You will have to train in special equipment such as fins and boots, both of which will take time for you to get adjusted to. Starting early is vital and it is best if you consult an expert first to help you with both aspects.

Remember that SEAL training is not going to be a walk in the park. You have to put in a lot of effort to secure yourself the position. Patience and hard work are the only two virtues that will help you sail past these sessions.

CONCLUSION:

Congratulations! You now know what makes Navy SEALs the best and can start training like one physically, mentally, emotionally, and nutritionally and be a more confident man. Yes, you may not become as tough as actual Navy SEALs but you can become confident enough to succeed in life using the same principles they use to win in just about any situation.

If there is one thing which can be underlined as the ultimate truth in this book, it is that the Navy SEALs are walking proof that the limits of what is humanly possible can be pushed much further than any one man can even begin to imagine. We have discussed their agonizing training in great detail, showing not only how far one can go, but also how far he can be *willing* to go for a worthy goal. The gist of the matter is, indeed, that will and what it can accomplish in the most hellish of conditions, let alone in daily life.

Further exemplifying the virtues of dedication and sacrifice are the real life stories we have touched upon through our chapters. None of us are likely to experience the horror and misery of war over the course of our lives, but we have a lot to learn from those who willingly step into the fray not only for their comrades and the objective but so that others don't have to do it. Try to imagine the kind of character that adorns a man who gives up everything, ultimately his life, for another.

While opportunities for such deeds may be plentiful in war, they are not common in regular, civilian life. All that is expected of us is to give such dedication and determination to ourselves and to our loved ones. But, don't forget that it always starts with you. It is only after you have mastered and began truly caring for yourself that you can be of service to those around you. Hopefully, this book has taught you just that and will help you take the first step on your way towards thriving and seeing great success in life.

Just remember that knowing is just half the battle and the other half is application. As such, I encourage you to start applying what you learned as soon as possible because when it comes to changing your life for the better, haste doesn't make waste. It helps.

After all, you're the only one who can take that first step. Nobody can ever take it for you. Nothing in life will come on its own, out of the clear blue skies, you have to seize the opportunities or make your own if life isn't throwing any your way. The same way that Navy SEALs become masters of combat and circumstance, trained to tip the balance in their favor and come out as winners, you must also do so in life. Attitude is where it all begins; your outlook is the canvas on which you paint your future, and the better the canvas the smoother and clearer the painting will be. As another prominent special operations unit, the British Special Air Service, has put so well in their motto: "Who dares, wins."

Here's to your becoming an ultimate warrior in life!

Finally, we would like to ask you to give a short, honest, and unbiased review of this book.

[CLICK HERE TO LEAVE A REVIEW](#)

Please & thank you!

Instant Access to Free Book Package!

As a thank you for the purchase of this book, I want to offer you some more material. We collaborate with multiple other authors specializing in various fields. We have best-selling, master writers in history, biographies, DIY projects, home improvement, arts & crafts and much more! **We make a promise to you to deliver at least 4 books a week in different genres, a value of $20-30, for FREE!**

All you need to do is sign up your email here at http://nextstopsuccess.net/freebooks/ to join our Book Club. You will get weekly notification for more free books, courtesy of the First Class Book Club.

As a special thank you, we don't want you to wait until next week for these 4 free books. We want to give you 4 **RIGHT NOW**.

Here's what you will be getting:
1. A fitness book called "BOSU Workout Routine Made Easy!"
2. A book on Jim Rohn, a master life coach: "The Best of Jim Rohn: Lessons for Life Changing Success"
3. A detailed biography on Conan O'Brien, a favorite late night TV show host.
4. A World War 2 Best Selling box set (2 books in 1!): "The Third Reich: Nazi Rise & Fall + World War 2: The Untold Secrets of Nazi Germany".

To get instant access to this free ebook package (a value of $25), and weekly free material, all you need to do is click the link below:

http://nextstopsuccess.net/freebooks/

Made in the USA
Lexington, KY
10 May 2016